A WILD PECULIAR JOY

BOOKS BY IRVING LAYTON

Here and Now   1945
Now Is the Place   1948
The Black Huntsmen   1951
Cerberus (with Louis Dudek & Raymond Souster)   1952
Love the Conqueror Worm   1953
In the Midst of My Fever   1954
The Long Pea-Shooter   1954
The Blue Propeller   1955
The Cold Green Element   1955
Music on a Kazoo   1956
The Bull Calf and Other Poems   1956
The Improved Binoculars   1956
A Laughter in the Mind   1958
A Red Carpet for the Sun   1959
The Swinging Flesh (Poems and Stories)   1961
Balls for a One-Armed Juggler   1963
The Laughing Rooster   1964
Collected Poems   1965
Periods of the Moon   1967
The Shattered Plinths   1968
Selected Poems   1969
The Whole Bloody Bird   1969
Nail Polish   1971
The Collected Poems of Irving Layton   1971
Engagements: Prose of Irving Layton   1972
Lovers and Lesser Men   1973
Seventy-Five Greek Poems   1974
The Pole-Vaulter   1974
The Darkening Fire   1975
The Unwavering Eye   1975
For My Brother Jesus   1976
Taking Sides (Prose)   1977
The Covenant   1977
The Poems of Irving Layton   1977
The Uncollected Poems of Irving Layton   1977
The Tightrope Dancer   1978
Droppings from Heaven   1979
An Unlikely Affair   1980
For My Neighbours in Hell   1980
The Love Poems of Irving Layton   1980
Europe and Other Bad News   1981
A Wild Peculiar Joy   1982 (1989, 2004)
The Gucci Bag   1983
Waiting for the Messiah (Prose)   1985
Dance with Desire   1986
Final Reckoning   1987
Fortunate Exile   1987
Fornalutx   1991

IRVING LAYTON

THE SELECTED POEMS

A WILD PECULIAR JOY

With an introduction by Sam Solecki

McCLELLAND & STEWART

Originally published in 1982
Expanded edition published in 1989
This edition published 2004

National Library of Canada Cataloguing in Publication

Layton, Irving, 1912-
A wild peculiar joy : selected poems / Irving Layton ;
introduction by Sam Solecki.

ISBN 978-0-7710-4948-4

I. Title.

PS8523.A95A6 2004   c811'.54   C2003-906718-1

We acknowledge the financial support of the Government of Canada through the
Book Publishing Industry Development Program and that of the Government of
Ontario through the Ontario Media Development Corporation's Ontario Book
Initiative. We further acknowledge the support of the Canada Council for the Arts
and the Ontario Arts Council for our publishing program.

The prose passages in "Irving Layton on Poetry," selected by Sam Solecki, are taken
from *Engagements: The Prose of Irving Layton* (1972), *Waiting for the Messiah* (1985),
and *Wild Gooseberries: The Selected Letters of Irving Layton* (1989), and are used by
permission of the author.

Typeset in Goudy by M&S, Toronto
Printed and bound in the USA

McClelland & Stewart,
a division of Random House of Canada Limited
One Toronto Street
Toronto, Ontario
M5C 2V6
www.mcclelland.com

5 6 7   21 20

With love, for
Samantha Clara Layton

CONTENTS

INTRODUCTION

From the early 1950s to the mid-1970s, Irving Layton was the most popular and most controversial poet in Canada. A critical buzz and often hostile reviews accompanied the publication of each of his collections of poetry, while his public readings attracted capacity audiences often in the hundreds. He was a star attraction, and Canada had seen nothing like his readings since Bliss Carman's national tours in the 1920s and E.J. Pratt's in the 1940s. I heard him read three times during this period and each time I had the impression of a man in his element – "me happiest when I [read] poems" – for whom few things held as much pleasure as seeing his poetry move people. Though his popularity was based on the fact that he was writing original poems of remarkable profundity and power – "The Birth of Tragedy," "The Cold Green Element" – he also had a reputation beyond poetry circles as an often abrasive and polemical commentator on culture and society. Thus even if you knew nothing else about Layton, you probably knew from his combative letters to newspapers and from the television program *Fighting Words* that he was the *enfant terrible* of Canadian literature. Some of this reputation was the result, he readily admits in his letters, of deliberate provocations against the Canadian establishment to get a hearing for his views in what he considered a still colonial country. That he was successful I can attest from personal experience. When in 1964 I showed my grade thirteen English teacher at Niagara Falls Collegiate Vocational Institute a copy of *Balls for a One-Armed Juggler* she commented that, unlike most major poets, he used four-letter words and his poems were often about sex. What she and I didn't know is that Layton had already answered that charge a decade earlier in a letter to Robert Creeley: "For this country the shits and pisses etc., the sex and scatology are a necessary antidote to the prevalent gentility and false idealism. Aside from the purely local and geographical I am convinced that the only protest, the only effective protest that a man can make today to the pressures seeking to annihilate him either physically or spiritually is the biological one. It is for our time that the paradox is reserved that the soul must be saved by the body, the highest by the lowest." In fact, the once forbidden words are as infrequent in Layton as they are in D.H. Lawrence or James Joyce, but they are the most obvious aspect of an often polemical poetry that sets out to challenge readers, in a way that no Canadian poetry had ever done, to a radical re-examination of the way they live.

Layton was part of the remarkable 1940s Montreal poetry scene that included F.R. Scott, A.M. Klein, John Sutherland, Louis Dudek, Patrick Anderson, P.K. Page, and Phyllis Webb. Though they differed on many issues and gathered around two opposed magazines, *Preview* and *First Statement*, they were united by a desire to bring Canadian poetry and society into the modern era. This meant responding to what was happening in Europe and the United States while jettisoning much of the inherited Canadian poetic baggage and contemporary provincial attitudes and values. Like poets of every era, they wanted poetry to use the language of its time in forms and conventions adequate to their complex historical situation. Almost all of them reached adulthood during the Depression and the Second World War. These, together with the Spanish Civil War and events in the Soviet Union, caused many writers, especially on the Left, to think of literature as a potential agent of social change. To adapt Marx's famous eleventh thesis on Feuerbach, they wondered whether poetry should go beyond interpreting the world and try to change it. In Layton's version, "there were just two kinds of people worth thinking about: those who were willing to die for a beautiful phrase, for a metaphor, and those eager to shed blood for a cause. Only at rare times was I confused about where I belonged. But the confusion, when I felt it, was painful, leaving me disorganized and robbed of volition."

He may not have joined those "eager to shed blood for a cause," but the 1930s idea of a poetry marked by or committed to a cause stayed with him.

None of Layton's contemporaries found the Canadian cultural tradition useful, and they knew that the neo-Victorian narratives of Pratt, the era's most popular poet, were a dead end. Layton sums up the situation in his 1985 memoir, *Waiting for the Messiah*. He points out that when he attended Macdonald College in Montreal, "Culturally, I might as well have been on the moon. There was no literary tradition in Canada. No authors, no books that you could talk about. Imperialists in Canada had done a thorough job of attenuating whatever feelings and ideas we might have had about our own country. Our cultural cupboard had deliberately been kept bare." It's worth recalling that as late as 1955, the *Times Literary Supplement* named Mazo de la Roche the greatest living Canadian writer. Not surprisingly, Layton referred to her dismissively as Mazola Roche. He knew the second-rate when he read it.

He is equally disparaging of the situation of the Canadian poet in his era. He writes in 1963 to the Toronto critic Milton Wilson: "The problem for the Canadian poet is a very difficult one. He's removed from the great issues of the day: his dilemmas are unimportant and derivative. He cannot know the men of action, the movers and shakers of history, as Shakespeare knew the Raleighs and Essexes – certainly not on the college campus! History and geography have both condemned him to be a minor poet." At best, as Hugh Kenner suggests, Canada offered Layton a situation without a tradition. Other writers in the same situation – MacLennan, Scott, and Purdy – found sustenance in Canadian history and in the Canadian landscape. History and nature are central to Layton's poetry, but never as *Canadian* history or landscape. For someone nurtured on the Marxist tradition of dialectical thinking, however, Layton never seems to realize that the lack of a tradition – Roumanian, Jewish, or English – might also have been a passport to freedom for him since the past was not a burden with which he needed to negotiate terms. In other words, he was spared the anxiety of influence that poets born into a major tradition inevitably experience; think of Larkin looking over his shoulder at Hardy and Yeats. Born Israel Lazarovitch in Roumania, Layton emigrated with his family to Canada in 1913; his mother's impatience with his father's piety distanced him during his youth from Judaic culture; and his status as an English-speaking Jew in Catholic Quebec prevented any significant contact with French literature. Canada did give him, however, a language and, in its schools and libraries, exposure to the rich and complex traditions of English and American poetry. His subject matter he would find through his reading, his life and in his gradual re-immersion in his Jewish heritage.

Boris Pasternak said that he admired Tolstoy and Dostoevsky because they had something to say about large personal, spiritual, and historical issues. Layton, I want to suggest, is one of those poets like Lawrence, Neruda, and Miłosz impatient with the traditional limits of lyric poetry precisely because he has something to say. This doesn't mean that we don't find in his body of work self-contained poems of concentrated authority, formal certainty, and figurative brilliance. "The Swimmer," "The Birth of Tragedy," and "The Cold Green Element" are there to remind us of his mastery of lyrics that resemble Keats's "well-wrought urn." At the same time, we almost always sense that many poems have metaphysical ambitions and that their voice, often addressed to us, directs our attention to a variety of issues at play in our lives. It's arguable that we can classify poets on the basis of whether they agree or disagree with Auden's comment that "poetry makes nothing happen." Rilke, Valéry, Mandelstam, Stevens, and Ashbery would be in the first category; Whitman, Lawrence, MacDiarmid, and Neruda in the second. While there's no doubt that many of Layton's major lyrics belong with the work of the first group, the limits of lyric as well as his rage against modernity regularly nudge him toward the second. As Eli Mandel points out, one of the unresolved tensions in the poems involves the struggle between the poet who wants to transform reality with his imagination and the poet who wants to dominate it with rhetoric and ideology. Layton's ambivalence, his desire for both, produces a recurring tension in his poems between the claims of life and those of art. Any poetry that overemphasizes the latter – think of A.J.M. Smith and Stevens – allows the discussion of life's major issues to be dominated by "reality doctors" (Saul Bellow's phrase) in media, government, or academy, and therefore acquiesces in values that have produced a deeply troubled civilization.

Whether as a dynamic, inspiring and much-loved high-school and university teacher or as a very public poet, Layton has been a resistance movement against middle-class values, conformity, inauthenticity, and anything that opposes human diversity and vitality. I once saw him in action in a classroom bringing to life, on a cold January afternoon, a group of fourth-year English students. We had finished a late lunch, and he asked me what I was going to do. I answered that I had my senior seminar on Marxism and Literature. He asked if he could come along. That day's topic was Alexander Pope, and Layton offered to lead the discussion about Pope's poetry as well as the poet's relationship to society in the eighteenth century. His brief lecture held the students spellbound and segued into a lively discussion that ended two hours later in a pub. He was seventy years old and one of the most famous literary figures in Canada, but he treated the students as equals in a spirited dialogue about their lives, literature, and what might be called the fate of the West. He was a one-man open university.

This openness and generosity of spirit have also been evident in his relationships with younger writers. Leonard Cohen, Eli Mandel, and Al Purdy are only three of many he helped to find their own voices with warm-hearted encouragement and tutelage. Purdy often referred to Layton as one of the two most important influences on his work (D.H. Lawrence was the other), and in a late letter even goes so far as to say that he "loved Layton" in the 1950s. Mandel showed his gratitude by writing the first – and still most perceptive – book about his work, *Irving Layton*.

Layton learned very early that if poetry is to make something happen, if it is to effect personal, social, or historical change, then not only must it speak the language of its age, but it must also be open to every aspect of reality, no matter whether it violates traditional notions of literary decorum or of what is appropriate in lyric. This may have been news in Canada in the 1940s and 50s, but it had already been taken for granted elsewhere, including in the poetry of Lawrence and Neruda. One can see it in the latter's call for a "poetry as impure as a suit or a body, a poetry stained by food and shame, a poetry with wrinkles, observations, dreams, waking, prophecies, declarations of love and hatred, beasts, blows, idylls, manifestos, denials, doubts, affirmations, taxes." In other words, a poem can be about anything, no matter how trivial, mundane, offensive or horrific: "The Mosquito," "Golfers," "The Skull," "The Fertile Muck," "Dracula," "The Cockroach" "Zucchini," "For My Brother Jesus," "Xianity," "To the Victims of the Holocaust," "Reingemacht." All of these offer the possibility of aesthetic pleasure in "the world's tangled and hieroglyphic beauty." Although Layton has a fundamentally tragic view of life and is one of our finest elegists (see "Keine Lazarovitch 1870-1959"), there are few bodies of poetry that so consistently celebrate life in all its diversity and rich contingent materiality. Layton also celebrates the importance of human differences and the free, spontaneous unfolding of the full individual in an increasingly rationalized, conformist and alienated mass civilization. But if the poems show a protean multiplicity, they are united by an underlying vitalism, a belief in life itself as a positive value. A poem embodies and expresses life. To Hölderlin's question, "What are poets for in a destitute time?" Layton answers, "in the creative word lies redemption" and

> Utterance alone can heal the ailing spirit
> and make man and poet a single self;
> bring back on the long vein of memory
> the laughter and wholeness of childhood.
>
> ("The Carillon")

According to Layton, a poem results when he goes "about making trouble for myself. / The sparks fly. / I gather each one / and start a poem." This is a playful way of making the important point that conflict, whether as animated conversation, a lively letter, a love affair or revolution, is as important to his dynamic conception of the creative self as it is to Nietzsche's, Lawrence's and Mailer's, to name two figures who are seminal influences and a contemporary Lawrentian whom he watched closely. (Incidentally, Al Purdy writes in *Reaching for the Beaufort Sea: An Autobiography* that when he visited Layton at his home in Montreal in 1955, he noticed a shrine to D.H.L., complete with photograph and candle.) In the 1930s Layton was enough of a Marxist to think of the social conflict as between the proletariat and the bourgeoisie, and he knew his Freud well enough to think of the self as a site of a turf war between Id, Ego, and Superego. But his breakthrough poems of the early 1950s are written in response to the influence of Nietzsche; they present conflict in predominantly Nietzschean terms as between Dionysus and Apollo and their figurative avatars. Readers of this volume will notice that it opens with the Nietzschean "The Birth of Tragedy" and closes with the Hebraic "A Wild Peculiar Joy." It's as if Layton is suggesting that the Hellenic and the Jewish traditions are two of the essential sources of his imagination and of his way of being in the world.

One of the earliest tips of the hat to Nietzsche occurs in 1946 in a characteristically combative review of Bertrand Russell's idiosyncratic and uneven *A History of Western Philosophy*:

Dipping into *Thus Spake Zarathustra*, a great and amazing book, Russell comes up with that soiled dishrag about men being trained for warriors and women for their recreation. Of Nietzsche's fierce and troubled honesty, astonishing originality, wisdom, and acute psychological penetration, there is not a single word. . . . Only thugs, gangsters and poets, Russell thinks, have accepted Nietzsche. Yet *The Will to Power* is nothing else than a colourful description of life's exuberance. The mature tree must shed its leaves; to live well men must be robust givers, spending themselves generously. This is the central idea running through Nietzsche's works. His Master

Morality will one day be everyone's morality. It is one of courage, health, tension, and laughter. His gods are gods who know how to dance!

It's worth keeping in mind that in 1946 Nietzsche was still being tarred as a result of the Nazis' use (or, rather, misuse) of his ideas. Walter Kaufmann's *Nietzsche: Philosopher, Psychologist, Antichrist*, the first major study in English, would not appear until 1950. The qualities and values Layton described admiringly in the review are also those he has tried to live by and the ones enacted and expressed in the major poems of the 1950s and 60s in which a vision of life and a theory of poetry are co-extensive: "The Birth of Tragedy," "The Cold Green Element," "Vexata Quaestio," "Tall Man Executes a Jig," and "Love the Conqueror Worm." These are high romantic odes written in Layton's most intensely figurative style where ideas and themes dance into life through metaphors. Northrop Frye's comment on "The Cold Green Element" applies to them all: "No quotation can do justice to the intricate unity of the poem." They also answer Layton's wish to write "even one poem that speaks with rhythmic authority about matters that are enduringly important." Notice the double emphasis on craft and content. Almost anyone can address matters of enduring importance, but unless he or she does so "with rhythmic authority" the result will not be a poem. The work of the 1970s and 1980s – since the early 1990s illness has prevented the writing of new poems – occasionally disappoints because Layton has forgotten his own rules: "For me, rhythm and imagery usually tell the story; I'm not much interested in any poet's ideas unless he can make them dance for me, that is embody them in a rhythmic pattern of visual images."

Layton's poetry is also Nietzschean insofar as it celebrates life even as it offers a direct and unmitigated encounter with tragedy and what Shakespeare calls death's "all oblivious enmity." Though this assumption will become more tangled when he confronts the Holocaust, Layton has always believed that poetry affirms life not only despite its horror but even because of it. The poet, like the Nietzschean *übermensch* and like Nietzsche's reconceived Dionysus, responds to life in its totality with a "joyful wisdom," a stoic "unwavering eye," and a tragic heroism. Layton captures something of this in the last two stanzas of "Love the Conqueror Worm":

I pardon Nature her insanities,
The perversity in flesh and fern;
I forget her lecheries,
　　Her paragram:
Love the Conqueror Worm

And praise these oaks which bare,
Straining, the hoar
Frost on them, stand each winter there
　　Like courtly masochists
　　Whimpering "Encore! Encore!"

If we wonder about the value of such a poetry, Layton answers that it helps us to see life more clearly and therefore helps us live. Thus, in "Fellini" he praises one of his favourite filmmakers as follows:

Your felicity, when it comes, is more brief
than the bubbles you loose over these ancient stairs;
perilous is the face you were meant to bear:
by art alone to modulate human grief
into a cry so sad, so strange, men call it rapture.

The mention of Fellini reminds us again of how often Layton's poems ignore Canada and turn to Europe and its cultural tradition. Whenever he refers to artists and thinkers whom he regards as salient predecessors and contemporaries, they are always European: the Old Testament prophets, Catullus, Dante, Shakespeare, Blake, Heine, Nietzsche, Whitman, Rimbaud, Lawrence, Mandelstam, Celan and Fellini. This shouldn't be surprising if we recall that, thinking about traditions and canons, he wrote in 1973, "I have only one establishment in mind: / That run by Homer and Shakespeare." His attitude to history is similar. It's as if only large issues and "world historical events" really provoke his imagination. In contrast to Scott and Purdy, he finds the Canadian canvas too small and the stakes negligible. Had Layton been a cultural critic, he would have been George Steiner who once wrote an essay, published in an American journal, arguing that the United States had produced no artistic work of the first importance. So much for jazz, abstract expressionism, Whitman, and Faulkner.

Layton also resembles Steiner in thinking that the genocide of the Jews in the Second World War is the most important event of the twentieth century and perhaps in the moral history of the West. From the late sixties on, his poetic critique of western civilization focuses increasingly on the history of the Jews, Christianity and the nature of evil. In these poems Jews become the symbol of suffering humanity, and, to quote a sentence from Tsvetayeva Layton admires, "In this most Christian / of worlds, the poet is a Jew." The emphasis on evil seems inevitable for a Nietzschean Jew with an already pessimistic view of humanity. It's noteworthy that Layton rejects the Platonist and Christian view of evil as merely the absence of good: whatever its source, evil is autonomous and a permanent constitutive aspect of our being. No causal explanation will be adequate in the face of our general penchant for cruelty, anti-Semitism, or genocide. And Layton's poems don't attempt one. Instead, they offer a mosaic, each part evoking a separate emotion, attitude, idea, or event, the cumulative force of which is more intense than that of the individual lyrics. "For Jesus Christ," for instance, takes the form of an address to Jesus, sometimes described as a poet, telling him what his followers have done since his death. It ends,

> Your stoutest, most selfless partisans in Europe
> laboured nearly two thousand years
> to twist your Cross into the Swastika
> that tore into our flesh like a fish-hook.

The last two lines are a fine example of sounds (f, s, t/k) working on the reader's ear and creating a "rhythmic authority." Layton, like

Kierkegaard and Lawrence, separates Jesus from Christianity, the debased religion of his followers; the Dane contemptuously dismisses the latter as Christendom, and Layton dubs it Xianity. These are angry, scathing, lacerating, bitter, and sometimes contemptuous poems often marked by a Swiftian irony. At their best they reveal Layton in fine form as a writer of jeremiads and satires.

The poems specifically about the Holocaust are written under the shadow both of the event and of T.W. Adorno's troubling comment, which he later qualified, that "It is barbarous to write a poem after Auschwitz." By poem, Adorno means any work of art attempting to deal with a subject ultimately unspeakable and unrepresentable, what Eliot calls "an instant eternity of evil and wrong" that leaves a "world that is wholly foul." Think of Spielberg's *Schindler's List*, Polanski's *The Pianist*, or the lyrics of Sachs, Celan, or Layton. Adorno was originally concerned that in an era of mass culture, "even the most extreme consciousness of doom threatens to degenerate into idle chatter." Later he also drew attention to the possibility that the artistic success of a poem – its beauty – might be at the expense of and might distract attention from its moral dimension and the suffering that was its origin. Polanski's decision to use a muted chiaroscuro and Spielberg's to turn to black and white indicate their awareness of the issues implicit in Adorno's comment. Similarly, Celan's lyrics ("Fugue of Death," "Münich, the Stork Inn") approach the subject obliquely, figuratively, and with a palette dominated by black and white. A comparable stylistic restraint marks the memoirs of Primo Levi and Wladyslaw Szpilman.

Layton's approach isn't as radical as Celan's; nevertheless, many of these poems are written in a simpler, more concise, nearly lapidary style. Here, as in poems on other topics, one occasionally senses an impatience with any poetry that isn't "direct speech . . . each word like a blow" ("Zucchini") – an impatience, in other words, that is an implicit criticism of his own best work. I wonder whether his reading in the 1970s of Eugenio Montale's stylistically more prosaic later poems doesn't also underlie the turn toward a simpler poetic. Of course, he may have simply felt that he had gone as far as he could with the themes and techniques that had made possible the best poems of his major creative period. As is the case with Neruda's later work, the poems of Layton's final period often show recycled images and rhetorical gambits. And yet, again as with Neruda (and I would add Al Purdy), one finds lyrics every few pages that remind us of the poet at his best: the apocalyptic "Reingemacht," the obliquely personal "Old Men," the minimalist "The Lesson," the puzzled *hommage* "Bottles," the prose poem "Late Invitation to the Dance," and the elegiac "Etruscan Tombs" – dedicated to Dante Gardini – whose last stanza could stand for Layton's epitaph:

> Nothing endures forever,
> Your pain, my pleasure,
> the seconds bear away;
> our flesh, Dante, one day
> will be such golden dust
> as a storyless wind stirs
> in an empty vault.

Eliot suggests that every poem is an epitaph. But a poet's epitaph has an extra dimension in that it also expresses anxiety over the survival of his work, even if, as in Horace's "Exegi monumentum" (Odes III:30), it asserts its immortality. While it is too early to wonder whether Layton will have a room in "the establishment run by Homer and Shakespeare," the committee chaired by time that determines these things will have to take into account the following facts. He is one of the greatest Canadian poets (only Purdy, Avison, and Ondaatje are his peers) and he is one of the few Canadian poets with a foreign reputation. Second, he has produced a significant body of work and a number of first-rate poems that have regularly been anthologized and continue to receive critical attention. And, last and for me most important, he passes what Orwell and Frye call "the test of involuntary memorizing." After reading him, you walk away haunted by lines that have insinuated themselves into your memory:

Done forever
with the insult
of birth
the long adultery
with illusion

•

Only from rot
are new shining worlds
begot

•

. . . the fastidious copulation of spiders

•

Triumphant matador, night
flings his black cape across the sky.

•

. . . and her youngest sings
While all the rivers of her red veins move into the sea.

•

. . . on the shore the damned ones
Applaud with the vigour of bees.

•

The bewildered ghost-sounds, ghost-meanings of old men

Sam Solecki
Toronto
November 2003

A WILD PECULIAR JOY

And me happiest when I compose poems.
    Love, power, the huzza of battle
    are something, are much;
yet a poem includes them like a pool
    water and reflection.
In me, nature's divided things –
    tree, mould on tree –
    have their fruition;
I am their core. Let them swap,
bandy, like a flame swerve.
I am their mouth; as a mouth I serve.

And I observe how the sensual moths
    big with odour and sunshine
    dart into the perilous shrubbery;
or drop their visiting shadows
    upon the garden I one year made
of flowering stone to be a footstool
    for the perfect gods,
    who, friends to the ascending orders,
sustain all passionate meditations
and call down pardons
for the insurgent blood.

A quiet madman, never far from tears,
    I lie like a slain thing
    under the green air the trees
inhabit, or rest upon a chair
    towards which the inflammable air
tumbles on many robins' wings;
    noting how seasonably
    leaf and blossom uncurl

and living things arrange their death,
while someone from afar off
blows birthday candles for the world.

THE SWIMMER

The afternoon foreclosing, see
The swimmer plunges from his raft,
Opening the spray corollas by his act of war –
The snake heads strike
Quickly and are silent.

Emerging see how for a moment,
A brown weed with marvellous bulbs,
He lies imminent upon the water
While light and sound come with a sharp passion
From the gonad sea around the poles
And break in bright cockle-shells about his ears.

He dives, floats, goes under like a thief
Where his blood sings to the tiger shadows
In the scentless greenery that leads him home,
A male salmon down fretted stairways
Through underwater slums. . . .

Stunned by the memory of lost gills
He frames gestures of self-absorption
Upon the skull-like beach;
Observes with instigated eyes
The sun that empties itself upon the water,
And the last wave romping in
To throw its boyhood on the marble sand.

I fixing my eyes upon a tree
Maccabean among the dwarfed
    Stalks of summer
Listened for ship's sound and birdsong
And felt the bites of insects
    Expiring in my arms' hairs.

And there among the green prayerful birds
Among the corn I heard
    The chaffering blades:
"You are no flydung on cherry blossoms,
Among two-legged lice
    You have the gift of praise.

Give your stripped body to the sun
Your sex to any skilled
    And pretty damsel;
From the bonfire
Of your guilts make
    A blazing Greek sun."

Then the wind which all day
Had run regattas through the fields
    Grew chill, became
A tree-dismantling wind.

The sun went down
    And called my brown skin in.

Before ever I knew men were hunting me
I knew delight as water in a glass in a pool;
The childish heart then
Was ears nose eyes twiceten fingers,
And the torpid slum street, in summer,
A cut vein of the sun
That shed goldmotes by the million
Against a boy's bare toe foot ankle knee.

Then when the old year fell out of the window
To break into snowflakes on the cold stones of City Hall
I discovered Tennyson in a secondhand bookstore;
He put his bugle for me to his bearded mouth,
And down his Aquitaine nose a diminutive King Arthur
Rode out of our grocery shop bowing to left and to right,
Bearing my mother's *sheitel* with him;
And for a whole week after that
I called my cat Launcelot.

Now I look out for the evil retinue
Making their sortie out of a forest of gold –
Afterwards their dames shall weave my *tzitzith*
Into a tapestry,
Though for myself I had preferred
A death by water or sky.

Mid-August the frenzied cicadas
Apprise the scene-shifters
Where each prop goes:
    Where the dark empery of bush,
And where the spacious blossomers.

Now lofty for the spinning year,
For the stripling I see pass
Dragging the summer by the ear,
    The flooding sun,
And the green fires in the grass

I pardon Nature her insanities,
The perversity in flesh and fern;
I forget her lecheries,
    Her paragram:
Love The Conqueror Worm

And praise these oaks which bare,
Straining, the hoar
Frost on them, stand each winter there
    Like courtly masochists
Whimpering "Encore! Encore!"

Tired of chewing
the flesh
of other animals;
Tired of subreption and deceit;
of the child's
bewildered conscience
fretting the sly man;
Tired of holding down
a job; of giving insults,
taking insults;
Of excited fornication,
failing heart valves,
septic kidneys. . . .
This frosty morning,
the coffin wood bursting
into brilliant flowers,
Is he glad
that after all the lecheries,
betrayals, subserviency,
After all the lusts,
false starts, evasions
he can begin
the unobstructed change
into clean grass
Done forever
with the insult
of birth,
the long adultery
with illusion?

I have seen respectable
death
served up like bread and wine
in stores and offices,
in club and hostel,
and from the streetcorner
church
that faces
two ways
I have seen death
served up
like ice.

Against this death,
slow, certain:
the body,
this burly sun,
the exhalations
of your breath,
your cheeks
rose and lovely,
and the secret
life
of the imagination
scheming freedom
from labour
and stone.

I do not want power
And great wealth I never cared for;
Most people, when I see them running after these things,
Fill me with anxiety and compassion;
I am anxious about them
And about myself who must unavoidably deal with them
These sick people whom no one loves or understands,
Whom even the gods
     with their lovely waterfalls and mists
Have completely expunged from their memory

These ailing people are each other's death
Sooner or later they fall upon each other's swords
They die into each other without valour or pity
Or fold noiselessly into each other like grey shadows;
They expire quietly like poisonous mushrooms
On a forest floor
And are shrivelled up by the sun
Into a fine white powder waiting to make greater sense
In some other more fortunate duration

For myself I like nothing better
Than to go walking down the unpaved streets
With the sun for my constant companion;
I like the way the dogs greet the two of us
With plenty of tail-waggings, rushes, innocent barkings.
When the children lift their faces
Like delicate flowers to be touched lightly
I feel an emotion no saint, no, nor mystic
Ever felt before me at this arrangement of sudden glory;
Perhaps the humble grasses in the fields
Understand this whitest ecstasy,

And the bare trees in late April
Waiting patiently for their gift of leaves

At such moments, poor and powerless,
I am so full of blessing I think I could babble
The meaningless religious words, the formulas of contrition,
The bewildered ghost-sounds, ghost-meanings of old men;
And if I do not it's because I wish to startle the earth
Bored to death by the prodigal centuries,
Their white ashes combed by fierce winds
Like the streaming hairs of frenzied anchorites,
The yea-sayers of hammered conviction;
And because thereby, decked out in green and gold,
She gains a greater glory –
The finer triumph – to force this praise from me,
An atheist, shivering with blessed ecstasy

Wanting for their young limbs praise,
Their thighs, hips, and saintly breasts,
    They grow from awkwardness to delight,
Their mouths made perfect with the air
    About them and the sweet rage in the blood,
    The delicate trouble in their veins.

    Intolerant as happiness, suddenly
They'll dart like bewildered birds;
    For there's no mercy in that bugler Time
That excites against their virginity
    The massed infantry of days, nor in the tendrils
    Greening on their enchanted battlements.

    Golda, Fruma, Dinnie, Elinor,
My saintly wantons, passionate nuns;
    O light-footed daughters, your unopened
Brittle beauty troubles an aging man
    Who hobbles after you a little way
    Fierce and ridiculous.

I have studied history, he said.
I expect nothing from man
Save hecatombs.
C'est son métier. And ferity.

No longer perhaps to his own kind
But to the sulphur-coloured butterfly
And young seals, white, without defence –
To whatever crawls, flies, swims.

It is life itself offends this queer beast
And fills him with mysterious unease;
Consequently only half-movements
Delight him – writhings, tortured spasms

Or whatever can stir his derision
By defect or ungainliness
Or, maimed, flutters from weakness like a bird:
Say, a noble falcon, with splintered wing.

It is as if, killing, he looked for answers
To his discontent among severed veins
And in the hot blood of the slain
Sought to inundate forever his self-horror

Or like a sodden idiot who plucks
A thrush from a willow, grief in her green hair,
Throttles it to uncover the root of its song.

Let the gods who made him, pity him.

Pitiless towards men, I am filled with pity
For the impractical trees climbing the exhausted hillside;
Sparse, dull, with blue uneven spaces between them,
They're like the beard of an uncombed tolerant monk,
      Or a Tolstoyan disciple, circa 1890.

Below these, a straggler, a tree with such enormous boughs
It might have remembered Absalom, who dead
Put by the aping of his father's majesty;
And one lone cedar, a sycophant, stunted,
      A buffoon with sick dreams.

While all around me, as for a favoured intruder,
There's an immense silence made for primeval birds
Or a thought to rise like a great cloud out of a crater,
A silence contained by valleys,
      Gardes Civiles in green capes.

Nevertheless the Lilliput train trivializes
The tolerant monk, the trees, and this whirlpool of silence,
Though it fling over its side like a capitalist's bequest
A memorial row
      Of blossoming cherry trees.

And the highway which seen from my window seems
A suture in the flesh of a venerable patrician
In the distance falls like a lariat on the green necks
Of the untamed hills that raise like wild horses
      Their dignified, astonished heads.

All day the heavens have opened up
and it has rained rained rained
rained
with the maliciousness of a minor poet.

It's not my element; I cannot live with it.
Perhaps because my forbears were thrifty merchants
it dispirits me to know
so much excellent water
      is going to waste, is going under bridges
to serve an outworn metaphor, expending
so much effort to so little effect.

Snow I can take, if I have to,
if only because of the satisfaction I have
in supposing that snow
is what someone has done to rain,
his contempt for it published in a million white bulletins.

It has rained for three days and three nights
and the vegetation is lush and very green.
They say Ireland is like that, the green rolling hillsides
a brogue in your eye and a lilt in both ears.
But I have never wanted to go to Ireland
now that her great sons are dead
(real Irish giants – Shaw and Joyce and Yeats
– not mythical ones)
and each little green blade, a rosary around it,
saying a paternoster to the wind.

Ireland? More like Africa.
I'm afraid to peer under my armpits, I might find
          tropical ferns growing sideways; and my limbs
      have begun to feel thick and rubberish and tubular.
I have the feeling if I step on the floor
              of my room,
water will splash out of my ankles
as from an old water boot or water bag.

The rain makes numerous thunders in my head,
          but it could be the tom-toms
      announcing the white man's love for the blacks.

Help me, someone.

I imagine my body is the whole steaming
                  continent of Africa,
and millions of animals are squishing
through the torrential jungle rains inside me
but one lion in particular –
          I see him, the fierce proud beast –
roars, and roars again:
roars roars roars roars

LOOK, THE LAMBS ARE ALL AROUND US!

Your figure, love,
curves itself
into a man's memory;
or to put it the way
a junior prof
at Mount Allison might,
Helen with her thick
absconding limbs
about the waist
of Paris
did no better.

Hell, my back's sunburnt
from so much love-making
in the open air.
The Primate (somebody
made a monkey of him)
and the Sanhedrin
(long on the beard, short
on the brain)
send envoys to say
they don't approve.
You never see them, love.
You toss me in the air
with such abandon,
they take to their heels and run.
I tell you
each kiss of yours
is like a blow on the head!

What luck, what luck to be loved
by the one girl
in this Presbyterian
country
who knows how to give
a man pleasure.

MISUNDERSTANDING

I placed
my hand
upon
her thigh.

By the way
she moved
away
I could see
her devotion
to literature
was not
perfect.

When Love ensnares my mind unbidden
       I am lost in the usual way
On a crowded street or avenue
Where I am lord of the marquees,
And the traffic cop moving his lips
       Like a poet composing
Whistles a discovery of sparrows
About my head.

My mind full of goats and pirates
       And simpler than a boy's,
I walk through a forest of white arms
That embrace me like window-shoppers;
Friends praise me like a Turkish delight
       Or a new kind of suspender
And children love me
Like a story.

Conscience more flat than cardboard
       Over the gap in a sole,
I avoid the fanatic whose subway
Collapsed in his brain;
there's a sinking, but the madonna
       Who clings to my hairlock
Is saved: on shore the damned ones
Applaud with the vigour of bees.

The sparrows' golden plummeting
       From fearful rooftop
Shows the flesh dying into sunshine.
Fled to the green suburbs, Death
Lies scared to death under a heap of bones.

Beauty buds from mire
And I, a singer in season, observe
Death is a name for beauty not in use.

No one is more happy, none can do more tricks.
          The sun melts like butter
Over my sweetcorn thoughts;
And, at last, both famous and good
I'm a Doge, a dog
          At the end of a terrace
Where poems like angels like flakes of powder
Quaver above my prickling skin.

In the midst of my fever, large
    as Europe's pain,
The birds hopping on the blackened wires
    were instantly electrocuted;
Bullfrogs were slaughtered in large numbers
    to the sound of their own innocent thrummings;
The beautiful whores of the king
    found lovers and disappeared;
The metaphysician sniffed the thought before him
    like a wrinkled fruit;
And the envoys meeting on the sunny quay
    for once said the truth about the weather.
In the midst of this rich confusion, a miracle happened: someone
    quietly performed a good deed;
And the grey imperial lions, growling, carried
    the news in their jaws.
I heard them. So did Androcles.

From the height of my fever, the sweat
    ran down my hairless limbs
Like the blood from the condemned patron
    of specially unlucky slaves. Then, O then
Great Caesar's legions halted before my troubled ear,
    impartial in Time's double exposure.
My brassy limbs stiffened
    like a trumpet blast; surely
The minutes now covered with gold-dust
    will in time
Drop birdlime upon the handsomest
    standard-bearer,
Caesar himself discover the exhaustible flesh,
    my lips

White with prophecy aver before him.
But the conqueror's lips are like pearls,
        and he hurls his javelin at the target sky.

In the depth of my gay fever, I saw my limbs
        like Hebrew letters
Twisted with too much learning. I was
Seer, sensualist, or fake ambassador; the tyrant
        who never lied
And cried like an infant after he'd had to
        to succour his people.
Then I, disengaging my arm to bless,
In an eyeblink became the benediction
        dropped from the Roman's fingers;
Nudes, nodes, nodules, became all one,
        existence seamless, and I,
Crawling solitary upon the globe of marble,
        waited for the footfall which never came.
And I thought of Time's wretches and of some
        dear ones not yet dead
And of Coleridge taking laudanum.

Now that I'm older
When I see a man laughing
I ask myself: Who
Got it? Who did he do in?

And when he cannot constrain himself,
But the tears run down his cheeks
And he slaps his thigh
Repeatedly,
I become worried and ask:
How many? A whole city?

And when I see
A woman smiling, showing
Her well-cared-for teeth,
I think: Boredom
And lust, and note
The gathering imbecility
On her face.

I suppose one day
The sun will black out
And these creatures
With their ingenious contraptions
For perfuming and surfeiting their bodies
Will die.

In the meantime they multiply.

And that other event
Is more than a billion years away.

MAXIE

Son, braggart, and thrasher,
is the cock's querulous strut
in air, an aggression.

At sight of him as at the sound
of "raw" my mind half-creates
tableaux, seas, immensities.

Mornings, I've seen his good looks
drop into the spider's mitre
pinned up between stem and stem.

All summer the months grovel
and bound at his heels like spaniels.
All seasons are occult toys to him,

things he takes out of the cupboard,
certain there are no more
than two, at the most four.

I suppose, spouse, what I wanted
was to hold the enduring folds
of your dress. Now there's this.

This energetic skin-and-bones. You'll see,
he'll pummel the two of us to death,
laughing at our wrinkled amazement.

Yes, though his upthrust into air
is more certain
than delight or unreason,

and his active pellmell feet
scatter promises, elations
of breast and womb;

yet his growing up so neighbourly
to grass, us, and qualifying cobwebs,
has given me a turn for sculpted stone.

Who is that in the tall grasses singing
By herself, near the water?
I can not see her
But can it be her
Than whom the grasses so tall
Are taller,
My daughter,
My lovely daughter?

Who is that in the tall grasses running
Beside her, near the water?
She can not see there
Time that pursued her
In the deep grasses so fast
And faster
And caught her,
My foolish daughter.

What is the wind in the fair grass saying
Like a verse, near the water?
Saviours that over
All things have power
Make Time himself grow kind
And kinder
That sought her,
My little daughter.

Who is that at the close of the summer
Near the deep lake? Who wrought her
Comely and slender?
Time but attends and befriends her
Than whom the grasses though tall
Are not taller,
My daughter,
My gentle daughter.

She came to us recommended
By the golden minutes and by nothing else;
Her skin glowed, sang with the compliments
Which these same minutes paid her.

Her hair burned like a yellow fire
To celebrate the strange beauty of her face;
Herself, she walked unconscious
Of the need she started in us to praise, admire

The elegance we found in us
Like a vein of rare silver when we saw her;
But all our thoughts were caught in the compass
Of her royal arms and we sank down

Into the dark where the blood sings after dark,
Into the light because it was the light,
Into the clear valley where her body was made,
Her beauty had lain, now resurrected

Raised by the minutes which start, slay,
Their ivory hafts fiery with sun-motes
Which, crying, we seized to make an immortal ring
For beauty which is its own excuse and never dies.

THE BULL CALF

The thing could barely stand. Yet taken
from his mother and the barn smells
he still impressed with his pride,
with the promise of sovereignty in the way
his head moved to take us in.
The fierce sunlight tugging the maize from the ground
licked at his shapely flanks.
He was too young for all that pride.
I thought of the deposed Richard II.

"No money in bull calves," Freeman had said.
The visiting clergyman rubbed the nostrils
now snuffing pathetically at the windless day.
"A pity," he sighed.
My gaze slipped off his hat toward the empty sky
that circled over the black knot of men,
over us and the calf waiting for the first blow.

Struck,
the bull calf drew in his thin forelegs
as if gathering strength for a mad rush . . .
tottered . . . raised his darkening eyes to us,
and I saw we were at the far end
of his frightened look, growing smaller and smaller
till we were only the ponderous mallet
that flicked his bleeding ear
and pushed him over on his side, stiffly,
like a block of wood.

Below the hill's crest
the river snuffled on the improvised beach.
We dug a deep pit and threw the dead calf into it.

It made a wet sound, a sepulchral gurgle,
as the warm sides bulged and flattened.
Settled, the bull calf lay as if asleep,
one foreleg over the other,
bereft of pride and so beautiful now,
without movement, perfectly still in the cool pit.
I turned away and wept.

SEVEN O'CLOCK LECTURE

Filling their ears
With the immortal claptrap of poetry,
These singular lies with the power
        to get themselves believed,
The permanent bloom on all time-infected things;
Indicating the will to falsehood in the hearts of men,
The music in a pismire's walk, the necessary glory of dung,
        immortal coal of the universe,
Leibniz's mirroring monads, daybeams of consciousness

I see their heads sway at the seven o'clock lecture;
I imagine they forget the hungers, the desperate fears
        in the hollow parts of their bodies,
The physiological smells, the sardine cans, the flitch of bacon,
The chicken bones gathered neatly
                to one side of the plate;
Life is horrifying, said Cézanne,
                                but this is not
        what he meant who picked flowers blooming
        in the slaughterhouse; he meant the slit throats,
The bear traps smeared with blood, the iron goads,
    the frightened
        servant-girl's Caesarian,
And this planet dancing about Apollo,
        the blood drying and shining in the sun,
Turning to Titans, beauty, the Arts. . . .

My heart is parted like the Red Sea.
It cracks!
And where the cleft is formed
The BARBARI carrying their chromium gods
    on their sunburnt arms and shoulders
Ride on my nightmares, a hot desert wind
    pushing them swiftly toward these faces
    washed clean of Death and Agony;
God! God! Shall I jiggle my gored haunches
        to make these faces laugh?
Shall the blood rain down on these paper masks?
Flammonde, Light of the World, in this well-lit
    fluorescent age you are a failure, lacking savvy;
Gregor Metamorphosis, fantastic bogeylouse,
    you are without meaning to those who nightly
    bed down on well-aired sheets;
In the fifth row someone pulls out a laundered emotion
    and wipes his long, false nose.

At last the bell goes, Lear lamenting Cordelia, the wall's
    piercing cry. . . .

    You may grieve now, gentlemen.

Below me the city was in flames:
the firemen were the first to save
themselves. I saw steeples fall on their knees.

I saw an agent kick the charred bodies
from an orphanage to one side, marking
the site carefully for a future speculation.

Lovers stopped short of the final spasm
and went off angrily in opposite directions,
their elbows held by giant escorts of fire.

Then the dignitaries rode across the bridges
under an auricle of light which delighted them,
noting for later punishment those that went before.

And the rest of the populace, their mouths
distorted by an unusual gladness, bawled thanks
to this comely and ravaging ally, asking

Only for more light with which to see
their neighbour's destruction.

All this I saw through my improved binoculars.

At the end of the garden walk
the wind and its satellite wait for me;
their meaning I will not know
        until I go there,
but the black-hatted undertaker

who, passing, saw my heart beating in the grass,
is also going there. Hi, I tell him,
a great squall in the Pacific blew a dead poet
        out of the water,
who now hangs from the city's gates.

Crowds depart daily to see it, and return
with grimaces and incomprehension;
if its limbs twitched in the air
        they would sit at its feet
peeling their oranges.

And turning over I embrace like a lover
the trunk of a tree, one of those
for whom the lightning was too much
        and grew a brilliant
hunchback with a crown of leaves.

The ailments escaped from the labels
of medicine bottles are all fled to the wind;
I've seen myself lately in the eyes
        of old women,
spent streams mourning my manhood,

in whose old pupils the sun became
a bloodsmear on broad catalpa leaves

and, hanging from ancient twigs,
       my murdered selves
sparked the air like the muted collisions

of fruit. A black dog howls down my blood,
a black dog with yellow eyes;
he too by someone's inadvertence
       saw the bloodsmear
on the broad catalpa leaves.

But the Furies clear a path for me to the worm
who sang for an hour in the throat of a robin,
and misled by the cries of young boys
       I am again
a breathless swimmer in that cold green element.

And if I say my dog's vivid tongue
Clapped the frogs under their green fables,
Or the rock's coolness under my hand
Told me clearly which way the sun passed

And if I say in a clean forest
I heard myself proclaimed a traitor
By the excellent cones, for I thought
Where the good go, green as an apple

And if like our French grocer Mailloux
I lay these things on your white table
With a hot involuntary look,
And add a word about the first gods

I take satisfaction from your smile
And the inclination of your shoulder
Before the birds leave off their singing
And slowly the dark fills up my eyes

But when you stand at night before me
Like the genius of this place, naked,
All my ribs most unpaganlike ache
With foolstruck Adam in his first wonder.

Faces I too have seen in clouds
And on the walls of an outhouse;
And this morning I saw a frog
Deadstill, showing its moist grey
Belly to some twigs and dry straw;
And a young terrified grass-snake
That threw off M's and bright S's
At the exact ferns as it streaked
Across my black boot into sedge.

To begin with there are the mysteries,
Though Klee recommends character
And Maritain has one lattice
That gives upon a monastery.
They write well; moreover, Klee paints.
To make a distinction, I think
Then that the poet transfigures
Reality, but the traffic cop
Transcribes it into his notebook.

In any case I'm adjusting
My organs to the future. Lies?
No: Language. The great days of Liz
Are mere Marlovian bombast;
The truth is dung, bubonic plagues
And London a stinking midden;
The maids unwashed and credulous,
The men coarse, or refined and corrupt
Reading their folios.

Sure I've come upon calyxes
And calicos, and melonrinds,

And fruitstones that reminded me
Of the bleeding heads of soldiers.
I've sworn then by the blood and gall
Of Christ and shouted eurekas
Till seven beavers watered me,
Putting out the fires. I've prayed,
Prayed and wept like a lunatic.

So I come back to the white clouds
And the outhouse wall. One may see
Faces anywhere if one's not proud.
The big words? I'd rather find lips
Shaping themselves in the rough wood,
Or connect my manshape's shadow
Floating like a fish under me
With – fish! Or think the day closes
Like the sad red eyes of your English cocker.

As a beginning, the small bird
And the small twig will do; the green
Smudge across the windowpanes
And the gathering dark; the insects
Outside, hungry, harried, hopeful,
Clamouring. As a beginning,
The bottles of amber ale, or the vexed
Stillness in the pioneer room
When no one spoke.

Then say, these were the gifted
Actors whose egotism, not green
Nor lovely as that of towering trees,
Broke the silences in the forest
Like a bulldozer. Smith, a mild
Eighteenth-century man, warm
And wanting praise, therefore not dead.
Frank Scott, proffering us the hard
Miracle of complexity
And humaneness, his face serpent
Benevolent.

And my proud friend,
Dudek, put out because the blades
Did not sufficiently applaud him
And the long-tailed thrashers ignored
His singing altogether.
A sad man. Rouault: *Le Clown Blessé*.
And Currie, drained of sex, a blight.
And other, littler fir trees giving
Their gay needles to the breeze.

All of them coughing like minor
Poets; all of them building
To themselves tall monuments
Of remaindered verse; all of them
Apprehending more of goodness
And wisdom than they could practise;
All of them, in word and act,
Timesputtering, foaming white
Like sodium chloride on water.

And then add this: though not trees
Green and egotistical making
Somehow a forest of peace,
Nor a lake dropped like a stone
Into the stillness which thereafter
Reproves the intruder in liquid
Accents; though no unsullen harebells
But a congregation of sick egotists,
We shall endure, and they with us;
Our names told quietly across
These waters, having fixed this moment
In a phrase which these – trees, flowers, birds –
For all their self-assertion cannot do.

Meek now as any Franciscan monk,
his inflated sac
    a minuscule bomb, a dark capsule,
he was in the exact centre
of the white writing table – a bull's-eye!
A white butterfly circled overhead.

What stupid extravagance, I thought,
to show himself in this fashion:
that dark loot outlined, letting the sun
betray him.

I crashed my hand down,
startling the gay white butterfly
that sailed swiftly on, then
licked the circle of blood
    on my palm to a crooked star,
faint, but one could decipher
it;

while the mosquito with a queer sort
of dignity clinging to its inert legs
trailed for both
                on the white circular table
a red flag of protest solemn
and useless.

Like Sieur Montaigne's distinction
between virtue and innocence
what gets you is their unbewilderment

They come into the picture suddenly
like unfinished houses, gapes and planed wood,
dominating a landscape

And you see at a glance
among sportsmen they are the metaphysicians,
intent, untalkative, pursuing Unity

(What finally gets you is their chastity)

And that no theory of pessimism is complete
which altogether ignores them

ON SEEING
THE STATUETTES OF EZEKIEL AND JEREMIAH
IN THE CHURCH OF NOTRE DAME

They have given you French names
    and made you captive, my rugged
troublesome compatriots;
    your splendid beards, here, are epicene,
plaster white
        and your angers
unclothed with Palestinian hills quite lost
in this immense and ugly edifice.

You are bored – I see it – sultry prophets
    with priests and nuns
(What coarse jokes must pass between you!)
    and with those morbidly religious,
e.g. my prize brother-in-law
            ex-Lawrencian
pawing his rosary, and his wife
sick with many guilts.

Believe me I would gladly take you
    from this spidery church
its bad melodrama, its musty smell of candle
    and set you both free again
in no make-believe world
        of sin and penitence
but the sunlit square opposite
alive at noon with arrogant men.

Yet cheer up Ezekiel and you Jeremiah
    who were once cast into a pit;
I shall not leave you here incensed, uneasy

among alien Catholic saints
but shall bring you from time to time
                    my hot Hebrew heart
as passionate as your own, and stand
with you here a while in aching confraternity.

A dull people,
but the rivers of this country
are wide and beautiful

A dull people
enamoured of childish games,
but food is easily come by
and plentiful

Some with a priest's voice
in their cage of ribs: but
on high mountain-tops and in thunderstorms
the chirping is not heard

Deferring to beadle and censor;
not ashamed for this,
but given over to horseplay,
the making of money

A dull people, without charm
or ideas,
settling into the clean empty look
of a Mountie or dairy farmer
as into a legacy

One can ignore them
(the silences, the vast distances help)
and suppose them at the bottom
of one of the meaner lakes,
their bones not even picked for souvenirs.

There are brightest apples on those trees
    but until I, fabulist, have spoken
they do not know their significance
or what other legends are hung like garlands
    on their black boughs twisting
like a rumour. The wind's noise is empty.

Nor are the winged insects better off
    though they wear my crafty eyes
wherever they alight. Stay here, my love;
you will see how delicately they deposit
    me on the leaves of elms
or fold me in the orient dust of summer.

And if in August joiners and bricklayers
    are thick as flies around us
building expensive bungalows for those
who do not need them, unless they release
    me roaring from their moth-proofed cupboards
their buyers will have no joy, no ease.

I could extend their rooms for them without cost
    and give them crazy sundials
to tell the time with, but I have noticed
how my irregular footprint horrifies them
    evenings and Sunday afternoons:
they spray for hours to erase its shadow.

How to dominate reality? Love is one way;
    imagination another. Sit here

beside me, sweet; take my hard hand in yours.
We'll mark the butterflies disappearing over the hedge
    with tiny wristwatches on their wings,
our fingers touching the earth, like two Buddhas.

At a distance, dark;
each as the philosophers
would remind us
a compendium of history.

Not like the dead bass
I saw afloat,
its history
what my eye made for it.

One bounces like a porpoise;
the tallest ones
race for the boat:
squeals, unself-consciousness.

But the youngest stops,
smiles at himself vaguely; at,
below the surface, the boulders
breathing like fish.

The sun is bleeding to death,
covering the lake
with its luxuriant blood;
the sun is dying on their shoulders.

SONG FOR A LATE HOUR

No one told me
to beware your bracelets,
the winds I could expect
from your small breasts.
No one told me
the tumult of your hair.
When a lock touched me
I knew the sensations
of shattering glass.

Your kissings put
blue waters around me.
I would look at you
with bold Cretan mirth:
I would forget
I am a cringing semite,
a spaniel suffering
about your tight skirts.

I slabber for your rippling
hips, your white shoulders.
I am sick
with love of you. Girl, o girl,
let our washed limbs make
a perverse Star of David
and cones of flesh,
Cythera all night
at my silvered back.

"I'm the sort of girl
        you must first tell you love."
"I love you," I said.
She gave herself to me then
        and I enjoyed her on her perfumed bed.

By the gods, the pleasure in her small
        wriggling body was so great,
    I had spoken no lecherous falsehood.
Now not I nor my beloved,
        such is our heat,
can wait for either words or scented sheet
but on her or my raincoat go roughly to it.

BARGAIN

In fourteen years
        of married bliss
not once have I been disloyal
to my wife;
and you, I am told, are still
a virgin.

If you are set
        to barter your maidenhead
for my unheard-of fidelity,
call me between three and five tomorrow
and it is done.

Her breath already smelled of whisky.
She lit a cigarette
And pointed to a flask in the glove compartment.
Then our mouths met.

She placed her hand on my groin;
She hadn't bothered to remove her wedding ring.
Her eyes closed with a sigh.
I was ready for the gathering.

You, Dulla, may prefer maidenheads;
But give me the bored young wives of Hampstead
Whose husbands provide them with smart convertibles
And who are reasonably well-read.

WOMAN

Vain and not to trust
unstable as wind,
as the wind ignorant;
shallow, her laugh
jarring my mended teeth.
I spit out
the loose silver
from my aching mouth.

With candid gaze
she meets my jealous
look, and is false.
Yet I am lost, lost.
Beauty and pleasure,
fatal gifts,
she brings in her thighs,
in her small amorous body.

O not remembering
her derision of me,
I plunge like a corkscrew
into her softness,
her small wicked body,
and there, beyond reproach,
I roar like a sick lion
between her breasts.

Mr. P. – I have heard it rumoured
That you, humanist, librarian with a licence,
In the shady privacy of your glassed room
Tore up my book of poems.

Sir, a word in your ear. Others
Have tried that game: burned Mann
And my immortal kinsman Heine.
Idiots! What act could be vainer?

For this act of yours, the ligatures
Pest-corroded, your eyes shall fall
From their sockets, drop on your lacquered desk
With the dull weight of pinballs.

And brighter than the sapless vine
Your hands shall flare
To the murkiest kimbos of the library,
Flashing my name like a neon sign.

And the candid great
Of whom not one was ever an Australian
Cry dustily from their shelves,
"Impostor! False custodian!"

Till a stunned derelict
You fall down blind, ear-beleaguered,
While Rabelais pipes you to a wished-for death
On a kazoo quaint and silvered.

ON BEING BITTEN BY A DOG

A doctor for mere lucre
performed an unnecessary operation
making my nose nearly
as crooked as himself

Another for a similar reason
almost blinded me

A poet famous
for his lyrics of love
and renunciation
toils at the seduction of my wife

And the humans who would like to kill me
are legion

Only once have I been bitten by a dog.

Whatever else poetry is freedom.
Forget the rhetoric, the trick of lying
All poets pick up sooner or later. From the river,
Rising like the thin voice of grey castratos – the mist;
Poplars and pines grow straight but oaks are gnarled;
Old codgers must speak of death, boys break windows,
Women lie honestly by their men at last.

And I who gave my Kate a blackened eye
Did to its vivid changing colours
Make up an incredible musical scale;
And now I balance on wooden stilts and dance
And thereby sing to the loftiest casements.
See how with polish I bow from the waist.
Space for these stilts! More space or I fail!

And a crown I say for my buffoon's head.
Yet no more fool am I than King Canute,
Lord of our tribe, who scanned and scorned;
Who half-deceived, believed; and, poet, missed
The first white waves come nuzzling at his feet;
Then damned the courtiers and the foolish trial
With a most bewildering and unkingly jest.

It was the mist. It lies inside one like a destiny.
A real Jonah it lies rotting like a lung.
And I know myself undone who am a clown
And wear a wreath of mist for a crown;
Mist with the scent of dead apples,
Mist swirling from black oily waters at evening,
Mist from the fraternal graves of cemeteries.

It shall drive me to beg my food and at last
Hurl me broken I know and prostrate on the road;
Like a huge toad I saw, entire but dead,
That Time mordantly had blacked; O pressed
To the moist earth it pled for entry.
I shall be I say that stiff toad for sick with mist
And crazed I smell the odour of mortality.

And Time flames like a paraffin stove
And what it burns are the minutes I live.
At certain middays I have watched the cars
Bring me from afar their windshield suns;
What lay to my hand were blue fenders,
The suns extinguished, the drivers wearing sunglasses.
And it made me think I had touched a hearse.

So whatever else poetry is freedom. Let
Far off the impatient cadences reveal
A padding for my breathless stilts. Swivel,
O hero, in the fleshy groves, skin and glycerine,
And sing of lust, the sun's accompanying shadow
Like a vampire's wing, the stillness in dead feet –
Your stave brings resurrection, O aggrievèd king.

My flesh comfortless with insect bites, sweat,
I lie stretched out on my couch of grass;
Chipmunks break like flames from the bleak earth.

And the sun's golden scarabs on the surface
Are aimless, nameless, scintillant;
Unmoving, or darting into pools

Of dark, their brightness gone. But the frog sits
And stares at my writing hand, his eyes
A guttersnipe's, leering. Or lecherous

As though an underworld savvy swelled
Those heavy-lidded eyes, xanthic beads,
They're desolation's self-mockery,

Its golden silence! Vacancy expressed,
Stressed by unblinking eye, fulvid lid!
And this vile emptiness encloses

Makes me too its rapt pupil. I goggle
At the quiet leaper, wondering
Will he rise up slim fairytale prince

At the first thundercrack? Will flash reveal
The universal lover, my Jack
Of hearts? A royal maniac raving,

Whirlwind's tongue, desolation's lung? Or flung
At the edge of this drear pool – mansoul,
Privity of evil, world's wrong, dung;

A cry heard and unheard, merest bubble
Under the legs of sallow beetles?
O, Love, enclose me in your round bead

O lift me like a vine-leaf on the vine;
In community of soil and sun
Let me not taste this desolation

But hear roar and pour of waters unseen
In mountains that parallel my road –
Sun vaulting gold against their brightest green!

Taking the air rifle from my son's hand,
I measured back five paces, the Hebrew
In me, narcissist, father of children,
Laid to rest. From there I took aim and fired.
The silent ball hit the frog's back an inch
Below the head. He jumped at the surprise
Of it, suddenly tickled or startled
(He must have thought) and leaped from the wet sand
Into the surrounding brown water. But
The ball had done its mischief. His next spring
Was a miserable flop, the thrust all gone
Out of his legs. He tried – like Bruce – again,
Throwing out his sensitive pianist's
Hands as a dwarf might or a helpless child.
His splash disturbed the quiet pondwater
And one old frog behind his weedy moat
Blinking, looking self-complacently on.
The lin's surface at once became closing
Eyelids and bubbles like notes of music
Liquid, luminous, dropping from the page
White, white-bearded, a rapid crescendo
Of inaudible sounds and a crone's whispering
Backstage among the reeds and bulrushes
As for an expiring Lear or Oedipus.

But Death makes us all look ridiculous.
Consider this frog (dog, hog, what you will)
Sprawling, his absurd corpse rocked by the tides
That his last vain spring had set in movement.
Like a retired oldster, I couldn't help sneer,
Living off the last of his insurance:
Billows – now crumbling – the premiums paid.

Absurd, how absurd. I wanted to kill
At the mockery of it, kill and kill
Again – the self-infatuate frog, dog, hog,
Anything with the stir of life in it,
Seeing the dead leaper, Chaplin-footed,
Rocked and cradled in this afternoon
Of tranquil water, reeds, and blazing sun,
The hole in his back clearly visible
And the torn skin a blob of shadow
Moving when the quiet poolwater moved.
O Egypt, marbled Greece, resplendent Rome,
Did you also finally perish from a small bore
In your back you could not scratch? And would
Your mouths open ghostily, gasping out
Among the murky reeds, the hidden frogs,
We climb with crushed spines toward the heavens?

When the next morning I came the same way
The frog was on his back, one delicate
Hand on his belly, and his white shirt front
Spotless. He looked as if he might have been
A comic, tapdancer apologizing
For a fall, or an emcee, his wide grin
Coaxing a laugh from us for an aside
Or perhaps a joke we didn't quite hear.

I put the cat outside to die,
Laying her down
Into a rut of leaves,
Cold and bloodsoaked,
Her moan
Coming now more quiet
And brief in October's economy
Till the jaws
Opened and shut on no sound.

Behind the wide pane
I watched the dying cat
Whose fur like a veil of air
The autumn wind stirred
Indifferently with the leaves:
Her form (or was it the wind?)
Still breathing –
A surprise of white.

And I was thinking
Of melting snow in spring
Or a strip of gauze
When a sparrow
Dropped down beside it
Leaning his clean beak
Into the hollow;
Then whirred away, his wings,
You may suppose, shuddering.

Letting me see
From my house
The twisted petal

That fell
Between the ruined paws
To hold or play with,
And the tight smile
Cats have for meeting death.

As if it were a faultless poem, the odour
Is both sensuous and intellectual,
And of faded onion peel its colour;
For here the wasting mausoleums brawl
With Time, heedless and mute; their voice
Kept down, polite yet querulous –
Assuredly courtesy must at last prevail.

Away from the markings of the poor
On slope and summit the statuary is vain
And senatorial (now the odour's
A high-pitched note, piercing the brain)
Where lying together are judge and barrister
And some whose busts look on a shrunk estate.

Persuade yourself it is a Warner set
Unreal and two-dimensional, a façade,
Though our mortal tongues are furred with death:
A ghost city where live autumn birds flit
And small squirrels dart from spray to spray
And this formal scene is a kind of poetry.

Especially the tomb of Moise Wong, alien
And quaint among French-Catholic names
Or the drainage pipes inanimate and looped
You may conceive as monstrous worms.
Undying paradox! Yet, love, look again:
Like an insinuation of leaves in snow

And sad, sad with surrender are the tablets
For the Chinese nuns; or, a blade between, the rows
Exact as alms, of les Sourdes et Muettes

And of les Aveugles: and this, dear girl,
Is the family plot of Père Loisel and his wife
Whose jumbled loins in amorous sweat
Spawned these five neat graves in a semicircle.

Like a socialist I knew, a simple soul,
These two sheep, male and female, stare at us
    from their fold;
And their faces are fine, fine and sensitive
With the proper intensity of reserve.
Even the credulity, so water clear in them,
    is attractive.

Yet, indifferent to the impression they make,
They crouch on their mat of dung or with the poise
    of a philosopher seek
The rough part of the post which they know well
To scrape against it their purloined fleece and fell;
Staring, warily staring, wearily staring, with a mien
    silly and gentle – and cynical.

Amazed? No, but look at those fine musicians' faces again;
More particularly, the ebony line of the mouth
    curving long and thin.
Do you see it? Would you not say that's the smile
You've caught and watched on the face of someone
    who, while he's too meek to defend himself,
Sees through and despises your guile?

I'll tell you something else about sheep
You haven't noticed, see them as much as you wish
    in your sleep,
They're neither this-nor-thats, half-and-halfs, if you prefer.
I've asked you to take in they scrub their fleece,
    standing rapt like a philosopher;
Their itchy, bulky, dung-matted, grey-dirty fleece
    yet, look down – what feet! the trim feet of a dancer.

And there's also this: they're practical, prudent.
Or they seem so, yet they also somehow contrive to appear
   gullible and vacant.
Here again is that unsatisfactory, disdain-making quality:
   that of the half-and-half, the in-between.
I should expect my gifted and temperamental daughter
If she flew high, then came down to failure
   to look afterwards as silly and circumspect
As this sheep and his dam.

But, Christ, the whole word moves in on this fold.
All, all, have become mixtures: alloys, neither
   pure tin nor gold.
Integrity's gone. And I myself at my wife's deathbed
Shall, I know, weep: weep like Othello, be
   grief-rent and troubled
Yet note the small cost of some extra flowers or bulbs.

That owner of duplexes
has enough gold to sink himself
on a battleship. His children,
two sons and a daughter, are variations
on the original gleam: that is,
     slobs with a college education.

Right now the four of them
are seated in the hotel's dining-room
munching watermelons.

With the assurance of money
in the bank
they spit out the black, cool, elliptical
melonseeds, and you can tell
the old man has rocks
but no culture: he spits,
     gives the noise away free.

The daughter however is embarrassed
(Second Year Arts, McGill) and sucks harder
to forget.

They're about as useless
as tits on a bull,
and I think:
Thank heaven I'm not
Jesus Christ –
I don't have to love them.

FOR MAO TSE-TUNG:
A MEDITATION ON FLIES AND KINGS

So, circling about my head, a fly.
Haloes of frantic monotone.
Then a smudge of blood smoking
On my fingers, let Jesus and Buddha cry.

Is theirs the way? Forgiveness of hurt?
Leprosariums? Perhaps. But I
Am burning flesh and bone,
An indifferent creature between
Cloud and a stone;
Smash insects with my boot,
Feast on torn flowers, deride
The nonillion bushes by the road
(Their patience is very great).
Jivatma, they endure,
Endure and proliferate.

And the meek-browed and poor
In their solid tenements
(Etiolated, they do not dance).
Worry of priest and of commissar:
None may re-create them who are
Lowly and universal as the moss
Or like vegetation the winds toss
Sweeping to the open lake and sky.
I put down these words in blood
And would not be misunderstood:
They have their Christs and their legends
And out of their pocks and ailments
Weave dear enchantments –
Poet and dictator, you are as alien as I.

69

On this remote and classic lake
Only the lapsing of the water can I hear
And the cold wind through the sumac.
The moneyed and their sunburnt children
Swarm other shores. Here is ecstasy,
The sun's outline made lucid
By each lacustral cloud
And man naked with mystery.

They dance best who dance with desire,
Who lifting feet of fire from fire
Weave before they lie down
A red carpet for the sun.

I pity the meek in their religious cages
And flee them; and flee
The universal sodality
Of joy-haters, joy-destroyers
(O Schiller, wine-drunk and silly!),
The sufferers and their thick rages;
Enter this tragic forest where the trees
Uprear as if for the graves of men,
All function and desire to offend
With themselves finally done;
And mark the dark pines farther on,
The sun's fires touching them at will,
Motionless like silent khans
Mourning serene and terrible
Their Lord entombed in the blazing hill.

BERRY PICKING

Silently my wife walks on the still wet furze
Now darkgreen the leaves are full of metaphors
Now lit up is each tiny lamp of blueberry.
The white nails of rain have dropped and the sun is free.

And whether she bends or straightens to each bush
To find the children's laughter among the leaves
Her quiet hands seem to make the quiet summer hush –
Berries or children, patient she is with these.

I only vex and perplex her; madness, rage
Are endearing perhaps put down upon the page;
Even silence daylong and sullen can then
Enamour as restraint or classic discipline.

So I envy the berries she puts in her mouth,
The red and spurting juice that stains her lips;
I shall never taste that good to her, nor will they
Displease her with a thousand barbarous jests.

How they lie easily for her hand to take,
Part of the unoffending world that is hers;
Here beyond complexity she stands and stares
And leans her marvellous head as if for answers.

No more the easy soul my childish craft deceives
Nor the simpler one for whom yes is always yes;
No, now her voice comes to me from a far way off
Though her lips are redder than the raspberries.

The large yellow wings, black-fringed,
were motionless

They say the soul of a dead person
will settle like that on the still face

But I thought: The rock has borne this;
this butterfly is the rock's grace,
its most obstinate and secret desire
to be a thing alive made manifest

Forgot were the two shattered porcupines
I had seen die in the bleak forest.
Pain is unreal; death, an illusion:
There is no death in all the land,
I heard my voice cry;
And brought my hand down on the butterfly
And felt the rock move beneath my hand.

I myself walked into the Sheraton
And after remarking his raw nose
Was part natal umbilicus I told
The clerk in the loudest voice I could bear:
"Page me Mr. Superman." He looked
Diffidently at me, but conceding
My tie-pin, made of the rarest onyx,
Belonged to neither a sour fanatic
Nor one sick in the head from eating
Shrimps canned in the Andes and contraband
Here, he signalled for a call boy who came
Running all spongy with awareness,
His cheeks flapping in the air-conditioned
Air and his white dentures extended in
Warmest greeting. "Page Mr. Superman,"
The uneasy clerk said, eyeing my pin
To reassure himself, and in his mind
Recapitulating the small number
Of paid two-week vacations he had had.
Luckily the grey-haired call boy was one
Of the ignatzes the cities now breed
Reliably and with a more exact
Efficiency than former days.
                               He saw
Nothing remarkable in the clerk's request
And sent his voice through the loudspeaker
Of his imagination constructed
In the faraway days of childhood in rooms
Alone with Atlas and the last pages
Of boys' magazines. I heard the glory
Of it that afternoon like the closing

Chords of Handel's *Messiah*. "Superman"
It rang out clear across the floor polish.

"Mr. Superman." There was such triumph,
Such wildest exultation in his voice,
The pale cigarette girl at the counter
For the first time in her life gave wrong change
And all the elevators raced upwards
As if a pistol shot had startled them.
They did not stop till they had crashed the roof
Where one can see their solemn closed cages
Side by side and standing pigeon-spotted
Like the abunas on the cathedral
Dazed-seeming by the wildest flight of all.

This was the cocktail hour when love
Is poured over ice-cubes and executives
Lay their shrewdest plans for the birth of twins
With silver spoons; when one forgets the ships
Aground in fog; the pilot with letters
For mountain peaks and snow; the silent poor;
Or the wife with pre-menstrual tensions;
When Asia is rubbed out with an olive,
A truce ordered to the day's massacres.
I saw only six in the large lobby,
Five men and one solitary woman,
Who hearing Mr. Superman called
Looked up at once from the puddle of their
Lives where they stood at the edges making
Crumbling mud pies out of paper money.
While the stout woman adjusted her bra
And studied the door of the Gents' Room,
The men had risen to their feet watching
Scared and breathless the quick revolving door
As if they expected the flashing blades

To churn him into visible substance.
But no one emerged from either place;
The unusual name was finally
Lost under the carpet where it was found
The next day badly deteriorated.

The condemned six returned to their postures
And the hour rained down the familiar
Wrinkles and the smiles cutting like glass.
The call boy gave it his verdict
Superman was nowhere in the lobby,
And the tall clerk now regarding my pin
Mistrustfully rubbed the umbilical
Part of his nose that was raw and itchy.
"He has not yet arrived," he said. "Perhaps
He'll come later." For a split second
I thought he was making game of me
But his eyes were steady as if fixed
On a T.V. serial. I thanked him
And smiling amiably in all
Directions of the bell-shaped womb, I walked
Out into the ordinary sunshine.

We were speaking of modern art.

"The human's no longer interesting,"
said the stranger.
"God, nature, man,
we've exhausted them each in turn."

It was a warm August afternoon,
and the linnet kept wiping its beak
on the fallen leaves and grass,
joyfully ignoring both of us.

As if he had done this
many times before,
the stranger dislodged the flat stone
near his hand
and let it crash down heavily
on the hopping bird.

Only the fluttering wing was visible,
and it looked
as if the ridiculous stone
was attempting to fly.

Then stillness: stone on wing; both partially
in shadow.
There was a sweet smell of earth.

"That makes an exciting composition,"
observed the stranger.

THE PREDATOR

The little fox
was lying in a pool of blood,
having gnawed his way out to freedom.

Or the farmhand,
seeing his puny, unprofitable size
had slugged him after with a rifle butt

And he had crawled
to the country roadside
where I came upon him, his fur dust-covered.

Hard to believe
a fox is ever dead, that he isn't
just lying there pretending with eyes shut.

His fame's against
him; one suspects him of anything,
even when there's blood oozing from the shut eyes.

His evident
self-enjoyment is against him also:
no creature so wild and gleeful can ever be done for.

But this fox was;
there's no place in the world any more
for free and gallant predators like him.

Eagle, lion,
fox and falcon; their freedom is their death.
Man, animal tamed and tainted, wishes to forget.

He prefers bears
in cages: delights to see them pace
back and forth, swatting their bars despondently.

Yet hates himself,
knowing he's somehow contemptible;
with knives and libraries the dirtiest predator of all.

Ghost of small fox,
hear me, if you're hovering close
and watching this slow red trickle of your blood:

Man sets even
more terrible traps for his own kind.
Be at peace; your gnawed leg will be well-revenged.

When I saw my mother's head on the cold pillow,
Her white waterfalling hair in the cheeks' hollows,
I thought, quietly circling my grief, of how
She had loved God but cursed extravagantly his creatures.

For her final mouth was not water but a curse,
A small black hole, a black rent in the universe,
Which damned the green earth, stars and trees in its stillness
And the inescapable lousiness of growing old.

And I record she was comfortless, vituperative,
Ignorant, glad, and much else besides; I believe
She endlessly praised her black eyebrows, their thick weave,
Till plagiarizing Death leaned down and took them for his mould.

And spoiled a dignity I shall not again find,
And the fury of her stubborn limited mind:
Now none will shake her amber beads and call God blind,
Or wear them upon a breast so radiantly.

O fierce she was, mean and unaccommodating;
But I think now of the toss of her gold earrings,
Their proud carnal assertion, and her youngest sings
While all the rivers of her red veins move into the sea.

I turn away to hide my terror
Lest my unmanliness displease them
And maim for all a half-holiday
Begun so well, so auspiciously.
They are building the mythical cage
Whose slow rise allows janitors, whores,
And bank presidents to display love
To one another like a curious
Wound, the Elect to undertake feats
Of unusual virtue. Masons
Give stone and ironmongers, metal
As if these were forever useless
In a paradise of leaves and sun;
And a blacksmith, handsome and selfless,
Offers to blind me at once without
Charge. A quiet shiver of self-love,
Of self-approbation runs through each
At the discovery of so much
Altruism – unknown, hitherto
Unsuspected – in their very midst.
The instance of the meek stonemasons,
The ironmongers and the selfless blacksmith
Seizes like a panic. Suddenly
Each one vies with his neighbour, avid
To seek out the more burdensome toil:
This one lugging spikes; that one, planks.
Affecting it is to watch their grace,
Their fine courtesies to each other
When they collide; or to imagine
Their tenderness in bed when they leave
The square littered with balloons, and me
Blinded and raging in this huge cage.

My son, said the repellent old man,
make certain you never need do
the dirty work of civilization.

All political credos, all religions
are necessary persuasions
to get the poor beggars into the mines.

That a few be whole, many must be broken.
All reform rests on hypocrisy:
fringe benefits for slaves and menials.

Fixed and eternal is the law of gravity:
so, my son, are injustice and the class war.
Living is an affair for aristocrats.

DIVINE IMAGE

Swiftly darting in the setting light,
The doomed sparrow feels the falcon's wings.

How beautiful are both in flight.

I

So the man spread his blanket on the field
And watched the shafts of light between the tufts
And felt the sun push the grass towards him;
The noise he heard was that of whizzing flies,
The whistlings of some small imprudent birds,
And the ambiguous rumbles of cars
That made him look up at the sky, aware
Of the gnats that tilted against the wind
And in the sunlight turned to jigging motes.
Fruitflies he'd call them except there was no fruit
About, spoiling to hatch these glitterings,
These nervous dots for which the mind supplied
The closing sentences from Thucydides,
Or from Euclid having a savage nightmare.

II

Jig jig, jig, jig. Like minuscule black links
Of a chain played with by some playful
Unapparent hand or the palpitant
Summer haze bored with the hour's stillness.
He felt the sting and tingle afterwards
Of those leaving their orthodox unrest,
Leaving the undulant excitation
To drop upon his sleeveless arm. The grass,
Even the wildflowers became black hairs
And himself a maddened speck among them.
Still the assaults of the small flies made him
Glad at last, until he saw purest joy
In their frantic jiggings under a hair,
So changed from those in the unrestraining air.

III

He stood up and felt himself enormous.
Felt as might Donatello over stone,
Or Plato, or as a man who has held
A loved and lovely woman in his arms
And feels his forehead touch the emptied sky
Where all antinomies flood into light.
Yet jig jig jig, the haloing black jots
Meshed with the wheeling fire of the sun:
Motion without meaning, disquietude
Without sense or purpose, ephemerides
That mottled the resting summer air till
Gusts swept them from his sight like wisps of smoke.
Yet they returned, bringing a bee, who, seeing
But a tall man, left him for a marigold.

IV

He doffed his aureole of gnats and moved
Out of the field as the sun sank down,
A dying god upon the blood-red hills.
Ambition, pride, the ecstasy of sex,
And all circumstance of delight and grief,
That blood upon the mountain's side, that flood
Washed into a clear incredible pool
Below the ruddied peaks that pierced the sun.
He stood still and waited. If ever
The hour of revelation was come
It was now, here on the transfigured steep.
The sky darkened. Some birds chirped. Nothing else.
He thought the dying god had gone to sleep:
An Indian fakir on his mat of nails.

V

And on the summit of the asphalt road
Which stretched towards the fiery town, the man
Saw one hill raised like a hairy arm, dark
With pines and cedars against the stricken sun
– The arm of Moses or of Joshua.
He dropped his head and let fall the halo
Of mountains, purpling and silent as time,
To see temptation coiled before his feet:
A violated grass-snake that lugged
Its intestine like a small red valise.
A cold-eyed skinflint it now was, and not
The manifest of that joyful wisdom,
The mirth and arrogant green flame of life;
Or earth's vivid tongue that flicked in praise of earth.

VI

And the man wept because pity was useless.
"Your jig's up; the flies come like kites," he said
And watched the grass-snake crawl towards the hedge,
Convulsing and dragging into the dark
The satchel filled with curses for the earth,
For the odours of warm sedge, and the sun,
A blood-red organ in the dying sky.
Backwards it fell into a grassy ditch
Exposing its underside, white as milk,
And mocked by wisps of hay between its jaws;
And then it stiffened to its final length.
But though it opened its thin mouth to scream
A last silent scream that shook the black sky,
Adamant and fierce, the tall man did not curse.

VII

Beside the rigid snake the man stretched out
In fellowship of death; he lay silent
And stiff in the heavy grass with eyes shut,
Inhaling the moist odours of the night
Through which his mind tunnelled with flicking tongue
Backwards to caves, mounds, and sunken ledges
And desolate cliffs where come only kites,
And where of perished badgers and raccoons
The claws alone remain, gripping the earth.
Meanwhile the green snake crept upon the sky,
Huge, his mailed coat glittering with stars that made
The night bright, and blowing thin wreaths of cloud
Athwart the moon; and as the weary man
Stood up, coiled above his head, transforming all.

By walking I found out
Where I was going.

By intensely hating, how to love.
By loving, whom and what to love.

By grieving, how to laugh from the belly.

Out of infirmity, I have built strength.
Out of untruth, truth.
From hypocrisy, I wove directness.

Almost now I know who I am.
Almost I have the boldness to be that man.

Another step
And I shall be where I started from.

I stand on a hill;
my mind reels in terraces
and I'm sucked into a whirlpool
of earth.
An evening wind rattles the almond trees.

In the hushed arena of the sky
the bloodied bull sinks down
with infinite majesty:
the stanchless blood fills the sea.

Triumphant matador, night
flings his black cape across the sky.

"Old man," I said, "it must be a trouble
To be bent as you are, nearly double.
So bowed are you, your forehead scrapes your feet,
Yet each day you parade along this street.

"Why are you not at home and in your chair
With wife or son to give affection, care?
What reason have you for disclaiming rest
When to stay by your hearth is wise and best?"

Slowly he straightened himself on his stave
And, scowling, this passionate answer gave;
Though he spoke, it's true, with such a muffled sound
His voice, I thought, must issue from the ground:

"You're not the first *señor* who on this street
Has informed me my toe and forehead meet;
Or bid me to take my quiet rest at home
And leave the bright streets for *chicos* to roam.

"I shall have a long time for my repose
Where one's feet are kept away from one's nose;
I say, before the eyes are shut; the tongue, mute
One should be all fingers – the world, his fruit.

"*Señor*, I walked as though I wore a crown
Till Time's *bandilleros* brought my head down;
Yet I'm not bent with seeking for my grave:
When I meet Death I'll strike him with this stave."

He raised his stick as though to strike at me;
Then lowered it with Spanish courtesy,

And putting one hand on his shrunken thigh
With the other – stave aloft – waved good-bye.

There was a pain in my throat; in my eyes, mist
For Death's frail, quixotic antagonist:
This pair of scissors made of head and limb
That cut, as he walked, the minutes left him.

From the place where I was sitting
I watched the weary stone-splitters
Building a road to blot out the sun;
And seeing their sweating bodies
In the merciless, midday heat
I wished I could do it for them:
Turn it out like a light, I mean.
And I almost rose up to do so
When my eyes suddenly picked out
A strange, never-before-seen worm
Making its way on the dried leaves.
It had a rich, feudal colour,
Reddish-brown like the Spanish soil,
And knew its way among the stones
So plentiful in Alicante.
I love lizards and toads; spiders, too
And all humped and skin-crinkled creatures;
But most in love I am with worms.
These sages never ask to know
A man's revenue or profession;
And it's not at antecedents
Or at class that they draw their line
But will dine with impartial relish
On one who splits stones or sells fish
Or, if it comes to that, a prince
Or a *generalissimo*.
Bless the subversive, crawling dears
Who here are the sole underground
And keep alive in the country
The idea of democracy.
I gave it a mock Falangist
Salute and it crawled away; or

Was it the stone-splitters frightened
The worm off and the brittle noise
Of almond-pickers? It vanished
Under a dusty dried-up leaf
For a restful snooze in the ground
But I imagine it now tunnelling
Its hard way to Andalusia
Faithful to the colourful soil
Under the villas and motels
Of those whose bankers let them stow
Ancient distinctions and treasure
In the rear of their foreign cars.

O plundered, sold-out, and lovely
Shore of the Mediterranean:
This worm shall knit the scattered plots
Of your traduced, dismembered land;
And co-worker of wave and wind,
Proud, untiring apostle to
The fragrant and enduring dust,
Carry its political news
To Castile and to Aragon.

The day you came naked to Paris
The tourists returned home without their guidebooks,
The hunger in their cameras finally appeased.

Alone once more with their gargoyles, the Frenchmen
Marvelled at the imagination that had produced them
And once again invited terror into their *apéritifs*.
Death was no longer exiled to the cemeteries.

In their royal gardens where the fish die of old age,
They perused something else besides newspapers
– A volume perhaps by one of their famous writers.
They opened their hearts to let your tender smile defrost them;
Their livers filled with an unassuageable love of justice.
They became the atmosphere around them.

They learned to take money from Americans
Without a feeling of revulsion towards them;
And to think of themselves
As not excessively subtle or witty.
"*Au diable* with Voltaire," they muttered,
"Who was a national calamity.
Au diable with *la République*.
(A race of incurable *petit bourgeois*, the French
Are happiest under a horse under a man.)
Au diable with *la Monarchie*!
We saw no goddesses during either folly;
Our bald-headed savants never told us
Such a blaze of pubic hair anywhere existed."
And they ordered the grandson of Grandma Moses
To paint it large on the dome of le Sacré-Coeur.

My little one, as if under those painted skies
It was again 1848,
They leaped as one mad colossal Frenchman from their *café*
        Pernods
Shouting, "*Vive l'Australienne!*
Vive Layton who brought her among us!
Let us erect monuments of black porphyry to them!
Let us bury them in the Panthéon!"
(*Pas si vite, messieurs*; we are still alive.)

And when, an undraped Jewish Venus,
You pointed to a child, a whole slum starving in her eyes,
Within earshot of the Tuileries,
The French who are crazy or catholic enough
To place, facing each other, two tableaux
– One for the Men of the Convention, and one puffing the Orators
        of the Restoration –
At once made a circle wide as the sky around you
While the Mayor of the 5th *Arrondissement*
Addressed the milling millions of Frenchmen:

"See how shapely small her adorable ass is;
Of what an incredible pink rotundity each cheek.
A bas Merovingian and Valois!
A bas Charlemagne and Henri Quatre!
For all the adulations we have paid them
In our fabulous *histoires*
They cannot raise an erection between them. Ah,
For too long has the madness of love
Been explained to us by sensualists and curés.
A bas Stendhal! *A bas* Bossuet!

"Forever and forever, from this blazing hour
All Paris radiates from Aviva's nest of hair
– Delicate hatchery of profound delights –

From her ever-to-be-adored Arche de Triomphe!
All the languors of history
Take on meaning clear as a wineglass or the belch of an angel
Only if thought of as rushing
On the wings of a rhinoceros towards this absorbing event.
Voyeurs, voyez! The moisture of her delicate instep
Is a pool of love
Into which sheathed in candy paper
Anaesthetized politicians drop from the skies!"
(Word jugglery, of course, my Sweet; but the French love it
– Mistake it in fact for poetry.)

And the *applaudissements* and bravos
Bombinating along the Boulevard Saint-Germain
Made the poor docile Seine
Think our great Atlantic was upon it.
It overflowed with fright into the bookstalls
And sidewalk *cafés.*
Fifteen remaining *allemands* with their cameras
Were flushed down the Rue Pigalle.

And when you were raised up
Into my hairy arms by the raving emotional crowds
Waving frenzied bottles of Beaujolais
And throwing the corks away ecstatically
(Not saving them!)
It was, my Love, my Darling,
As if someone had again ordered an advance
Upon the Bastille
Which we recalled joyously, face to face at last,
Had yielded after only a small token resistance.

The famous and rich, even the learned and the wise,
    Singly or in pairs went to her dwelling
To press their civilized lips to her thighs
    Or learn at first hand her buttocks' swelling.

Of high-paying customers she had no lack
    And was herself now rich: so she implied.
Mostly she had made her pile while on her back
    But sometimes she had made it on the side.

Reich she read; of course the Viennese doctor.
    Lawrence – his poems and novels she devoured;
Kafka at the beginning almost rocked her
    But as she read him more she said he soured.

Swedish she spoke, French, Polish, fluent German;
    Had even picked up Hindi – who knows how?
In bed she had learned to moan and sigh in Russian
    Though its rhythms troubled her even now.

A nymphomaniac like Napoleon's sister
    She could exhaust a bull or stallion;
Bankers had kneeled before her crotch to kiss her
    And ex-princes, Spanish and Italian.

And all the amorous mayors of France-Sud
    Impelled by lust or by regional pride
Would drive their Renaults into her neighbourhood,
    Ring her bell and troop happily inside.

And pimpled teenagers whom priests and rabbis
  Had made gauche, fearful, prurient and blind
Prodded by Venus had sought her expert thighs:
  Ah, to these she was especially kind.

And having translated several Swinburne lines
  She kept the finest whips she could afford
To be, though most aristocrats brought their canes,
  Ready for some forgetful English lord.

We saw waves like athletes dash towards the shore
  Breaking it seemed from a line of green scum;
We saw the sun dying, and this aged whore
  Noted how it gave clouds a tinge of rum.

Engaging was her mien, her voice low and sweet;
  Convent nuns might have envied her address.
She was touched by the bathers below her feet;
  I, by this vitality sprung from cess.

And as she spoke to me on the crowded quay
  And reminisced about her well-spent years
I mourned with her her shrivelled face and body
  And gave what no man had given her: tears.

An Indian chief steps out on the quay
and offers me the smell of balsam and fir;
he asks me to look at his wampum belt
and the beaverskin holed by French bullets;
he makes a sign as silent as his beads.
Though his face is bronzed and painted up
it is not unfriendly; just the same the tourists
– German, Dutch, Italian, Spanish, blond Swedes –
have no yen to meet him. Only an American
stays behind, sharing with me an affection
ancestral as our gloomy forests and lakes
for this misplaced Iroquois chief
whose grim, unexpected presence on the quay
throws a shadow over the sunbathers
lolling in their *fauteuils* and *chaises longues*
like that of pigeons startled by a sudden noise,
and over the luxury apartment buildings
on the Promenade des Anglais
that now seem made of plastic matchsticks
over which some fat, rich, and retarded boy
has thrown tinsel from a million cigarette boxes.

"Ugh, Ugh," the Indian chief says
with the utmost guttural expressiveness
so as not to disappoint the American and me
(but he may have merely been clearing his throat)
"This sea smells too much of espresso coffee,
also of love-making and imported whisky;
and look – there, there, farther off – no one swims
in it: those are not arms, they are *baguettes*!"
They really are the arms of a lone swimmer
who's ventured some distance from the beach

and the French provincials browning their pots
but I get his point. Doubtless this Indian
has picked up the Jew's love of exaggeration
or maybe the trait is Mediterranean
and the chief has spent his wampum money
getting to know other cultures than his own;
his irony gives me a charge
but since chromatic scars are overawing
I don't ask him where he's picked it up
and he takes my silence as a sign
that my enlightenment is now complete.

He moves towards the curb where sighting a Peugeot
he throws himself directly under its wheels;
nobody else sees this encounter of Indian
and car except the two of us
who tense for the explosion of beads and fur
that must fall on everyone's head like confetti;
but there's no explosion, no sound of brakes;
the Peugeot drives on as if it had hit a shadow
and the American and I go off to the nearest bar
to gulp one pony of firewater after another
and tell the young dazzling ash blonde harlots
admiring their Côte d'Azur suntans
and the fatbellies pricing them that nothing happened.

The castles on the Rhine
are all haunted
by the ghosts of Jewish mothers
looking for their ghostly children

And the clusters of grapes
in the sloping vineyards
are myriads of blinded eyes
staring at the blind sun

The tireless Lorelei
can never comb from their hair
the crimson beards
of murdered rabbis

However sweetly they sing
one hears only
the low wailing of cattle-cars
moving invisibly across the land

THE SKULL

Out of my wrecked marriages
disappointments with friends
the rime time deposits
on heart, imagination

And earth's magnetic pull
downwards to the grave

I want to write poems
as clean and dry
and as impertinent
as this white skull

Found by me
outside the small boneyard
at Mithymna

That perched on a cliffedge
stares
and grins at the sea

The tremulous moment he works and waits for
when the difficult poem is almost done
and demands only the fine transposition
of a single line, the smallest change in tone

Is the imperial moment just before
the blinding clap of ejaculation,
when he can still urge on his ecstasy
and ecstasy and fate are one

Is Helios waiting in the blue sky for
the zenith's inevitable hammerstroke
timed to fall on his brass gong
at the exact instant of plenitude and decline

The total white exquisiteness before corruption
when the wave's wide flaunting crest
with smash and tumult prepares to break
into bleak nothingness on Ithaca's shore

All afternoon she sits in the doorway, a tourist attraction
    to be stared at by Greeks or the foreigners
Who know her story. Old and ill and her feet swollen
    to rhinoceros size
Once, long ago, she was a wild creature so fair and disdainful
    she made the sober merchants dream at their tills
And fishermen haul in lascivious sea-nymphs all night long.
Their wives, even the comeliest of virgins, cursed her beauty
    praying their merciful God
To strike her with plague or leprosy. One day He lifted a petitioner's
    taper from its tiny brass socket
And turned it into a man handsome and clever with words, poet
    and talked-about novelist from another island.
She saw him and fell, his curious fire loosening her limbs;
In the crumbling Genoese castle, surrounded by ears,
    they made love.
The furious villagers rejoiced. At last the contemptuous beauty
    had been roiled in the mire
Her scented petticoats pulled over her head,
    her besmutted buttocks for all to see.
O the fetid dreams of men! How they besmeared the white breasts
    that had made them groan in their sleep
How they reviled what for so long they had longed for in vain
While the women and girls so lit up the church
With grateful candles you'd think for weeks God's face
    was shining there.
He lifted yet another taper and blew out its flame: the teller of tales
    made off for Athens to compose
A moving novel about their tragic love and never saw her again
But overnight she became the ruined unhappy heroine
    of a thousand lustful dreams
Such that aesthetes and bored rich women dream

And wandered from place to place to return at last
    comfortless and impenitent
To her village and the filthy leers of men, the compassionate jeers
    of wives and virgins
To live solitary and infamous in the house where you see her now.
All that was long ago. Day by remorseless day
Her famed and troubling beauty crumbled into commemorative
    moles, wrinkles and yellowing parchment skin
And the heartbreak of an old woman's toothless grin.
Now there isn't a villager, old or young,
Who doesn't run up to embrace this hairy misshapen crone
    with the wild gone look in her eyes
And the sour excremental smell that fills up her doorway.
Not one who does not feel glad and right
Having someone whom daily he can forgive and pity
Or whose heart is not made proud to fix her hoary and humbled
    at the end of his benevolent stare;
Especially since the government itself is rumoured to allow her
    a small stipend to sit in the doorway
    to be gawked at, an Aeschylean lesson for all Greeks,
Her fabled loveliness caught forever in a work of imperishing art
    while her dying decrepit self,
A tourist attraction in the village, puts still more drachmas
    in the merchants' tills.

For years
        I taught myself
the wholly impractical art
  of arranging words
on paper

And gave
        a respectful hearing
to sentimental utopians
   poets among them
as well as metaphysicians & moralists
discoursing on the human
   condition

Forgetting
        nature
plays favourites
and gives only
   to those who have:
the weak
        she pounds
into the earth
          to learn there
her lesson
   from worms & moles

Forgetting
        she's a deaf-mute
who's never   heard
   and who never
speaks
        of conscience & justice

Though
        wearing an enigmatic
smile
     she will allow
for a season
   the over-sensitive
     to mention them
in passing

Lord I understand the plan, the news is out:
I kill him, he kills me, change and change about,
And you ever in the right; and no wonder
Since it's no great matter who's up, who's under.
Teuton or Slav, Arab or suffering Jew –
Nature, Justice, God – they are all one to you.
The lion breeds the lamb and the antelope
As evil breeds good; darkness, light; despair, hope.

And though your scheme confounds theologians' wits
All come and go sired by the opposites;
And they decree: he who slays and he who's slain
Leave on your excellent world no crimson stain.
The tragic, warring creatures that here have breath
Are reconciled in the partnership of death;
And death's akin to art, and artists please
To the measure they have stilled the contraries.

Energy must crackle on a silent urn,
Nothing catch fire though Jerusalem burn,
And the lion poised on the poor bok to spring
Hold in his furious jaws no suffering.
Motion and rest, love and hate, heaven and hell
Here cease their Punch-and-Judy show: all is well.
There is no pain in the graveyard or the voice
Whispering in the tombstones: "Rejoice, rejoice."

FOR MUSIA'S GRANDCHILDREN

I write this poem
for your grandchildren
for they will know of your loveliness
only from hearsay,
from yellowing photographs
spread out on table and sofa
for a laugh.

When arrogant
with the lovely grace you gave their flesh
they regard your dear frail body pityingly,
your time-dishonoured cheeks
pallid and sunken
and those hands
that I have kissed a thousand times
mottled by age
and stroking a grey ringlet into place,
I want them suddenly
to see you as I saw you
– beautiful as the first bird at dawn.

Dearest love, tell them
that I, a crazed poet all his days
who made woman
his ceaseless study and delight,
begged but one boon
in this world of mournful beasts
that are almost human:
to live praising your marvellous eyes
mischief could make glisten
like winter pools at night
or appetite put a fine finish on.

A moment ago, in my embrace
She rode me like a Joan of Arc;
Then seeing my fifty-year-old face
Where Time's acids had burned deep their mark,
My head of hair coloured grey and rust,
And my old eyes wise with genial lust
She stiffened and held herself in check.

I felt her limbs slacken at my side
As sweetly she kissed my wrinkled neck;
Desire unspent had all but fled
Leaving behind its wraith, mere sentiment,
That poised her astride me motionless.
Ah, if my flesh were but firm, not loose,
And I were young, how she'd ride and ride!

FOR NATALYA CORREIA

You possess the sturdy elegance of a cannon
and move always with the authority
of someone about to capture a city

Are indisputably beyond the vanity
of attention and compliments
like famous statues fixed in permanent triumph

Who in aloof approving silence
or unending melancholy disdain
regard their admirers at the crowded base

If you dispense anger or annoyance
it is as if doing so you establish
the existence of those who provoked them

And entertain each day those certainties
acclamation and gratified desire foster
in a voluptuous and talented woman

I admire wholeheartedly the egotism
with which you half stretch out on your couch
like a glistening female sea lion

And pour without my permission
wine from my wineglass into your own
fanning with delighted self-absorption

The smoke curling about your impressive head
or jab into space your ebony cigarette holder
as if to poke emeralds from their hiding place

I do not know what Chinese dragons eat
but *Vipera russellii* in cages must be fed

On the soft mat of vipershit, godlike,
without compassion or malice
the famed nutritionist
released the white mouse
– cotton fluff with bright pink eyes –
and for a second only
the poor albino
turned to us his bewildered pink eyes
then shifted and ran around the cage
– the dancing, prancing little show-off;
ran with the heady stuff of life
in his ridiculous tiny wishbone legs,
at times raising himself against the glass cage,
standing there, white, like a splayed bat,
then fluttering off into the flecked shadows,
a piece of cambric in a sudden lift of air

Stung,
the white mouse reared up,
swayed and wobbled like a diapered infant
– the death quiver in his small buttocks –
then fell like a furred stone,
the four legs stiffening with eternity

The unhinged viper
swallowed him head first
and the last I saw of the mouse
was a poignant good-bye flick of his tail,
the soothing peristalsis

ending only when he rested
in the middle of the viper's length:
a pleasant, elastic, cosy bubble
lulling as the Madonna's lap after the Annunciation

And I broke into laughter
for this absurdity
and for the mouse's juices soon to begin
running the length and roundness of the viper,
for the flesh and fragile bones commencing
their inevitable transformative cellular dance

I laughed
as might any well-disciplined Zarathustrian
in this godless epoch
but that evening after I'd sown grass seed
in the round bald spot of my lawn
neatly circular as Caesar's empty pate,
restored the earth and watered it carefully,
suddenly when I was resting on the doorstep
I felt a tremor in my head and frame
as if a whole world had moved inside me

Like a mother demented nature caresses
her children before she chokes them to death;
she raises tall palmtrees and whirlwinds to crack them:
only by continually devouring herself does she endure.

Out of her immemorial dung come flowers and stars,
come gracious ladies with tiny troutbones between their teeth
or goose-fat on the tips of flirtatious tongues
– with animal perfumes on their cool adulterous wrists.

At a later hour, the gracious ladies fall into the earth
where graveworms nibble all day long on their delicate parts,
unaware how fallen breasts and vaginas once gave birth
to mediocre poetry, to ecstasies and sighs.

For you, my sweet, you and me, the human race entire
she invented to watch this tragic and strange affair
for who wishes to play Hamlet when the gallery is bare?
Mind, Mind was in the mind of that performer!

Now when lightning splits the high arrogant oaks
and mountains rise and fall, or lions and tigers prowl
or crippled poets run and win the coveted laurel,
man, her darling pervert, sees and notes it all.

But the cost, the cost of this ghastly privilege
is unendurable guilt that we dredge and dredge
as horrorstruck we find our condemned selves on the stage
beside her, nature's most murderous tool and accomplice.

Love, I kiss your navel and my x-ray eyes see
fisheyes wink in your dissolving entrails,
and when I write my lying poems know I am using
an anodyne from which the fastidious man recoils.

CENTENNIAL ODE

Like an old, nervous and eager cow
my country
is being led up to the bull
of history

The bull has something else
on his mind
and ignores her;
still, dazed by her wagging tail, in good time
he must unsheathe
his venerable tool
for the long-awaited consummation

Certainly it will be the biggest
bang-up affair
within the memory of centenarians,
and seismologists have been alerted
everywhere
to record the shocks and tremors

Emissaries
are fanning out to advise
younger and older statesmen around the globe:
take note, finally our brindled Elsie
is mating history

For everyone coming to watch
this extraordinary event
there can be standing room only
for himself
and a single bag of overcharged peanuts

Poor dear
what will she do
the day after
when she looks in a pool
and sees
the same bland face,
the same dull wrinkles between the horns
and the relieved bull
even more indifferent than before?

OSIP MANDELSHTAM (1891–1940)

I once did an hour-long T.V. show reading
from your *Stamen* and *Tristia*: out there
were my compatriots who had never before
heard of your name and pain, your nightmare fate;
of course the impresario spoke impressively
about your stay in Paris where you mastered
the French symbolists, your skill as translator
(what pre-Belsen Jew hadn't promiscuously
shacked up with five or six gentile cultures?),
the Hellenic feeling in your prose and poems
– to be brief, he filled in the familiar picture
of enlightened Jew, ass bared to the winds

But when that self-taught master symbolist
il miglior fabbro put you on his list of touchables
that was the end; you perished in the land waste
of Siberia, precisely where no one knows and few care
for in that stinking *imperium* whose literature
you adorned like a surreal Star of David
you're still an unclaimed name, a Jewish ghost
who wanders occasionally into enclaves
of forlorn intellectuals listening
for the ironic scrape of your voice
in the subversive hum of underground presses

I know my fellow Canadians, Osip;
they forgot your name and fate as swiftly
as they learned them, switching off
the contorted image of pain with their sets,
choosing a glass darkness to one which starting
in the mind covers the earth in permanent eclipse;
so they chew branflakes and crabmeat, gossip, make love,

take out insurance against fires and death
while our poetesses explore their depressions
in delicate complaints regular as menstruation
or eviscerate a dead god for metaphors;
the men-poets displaying codpieces of wampum,
the safer legends of prairie Indian and Eskimo

Under a sour and birdless heaven
T.V. crosses stretch across a flat Calvary
and plaza storewindows give me
the blank expressionless stare of imbeciles:
this is Toronto, not St. Petersburg on the Neva;
though seas death and silent decades separate us
we yet speak to each other, brother to brother;
your forgotten martyrdom has taught me scorn
for hassidic world-savers without guns and tanks:
they are mankind's gold and ivory toilet bowls
where brute or dictator relieves himself
when reading their grave messages to posterity
– let us be the rapturous eye of the hurricane
flashing the Jew's will, his mocking contempt for slaves

From my heart I rooted out Jehovah;
I spurned Moses and his Tables of Law
And tore up my father's phylacteries.
Did I turn from dragons to live with fleas?

The Lord of Israel hates injustice and lies.
Your father's end will be your own: apoplexy.
You'll writhe in agony though stiff as celery stalk.
Order your wheelchair now and save money.

ABSENCE

Love,
I make a silence
out of your name
and dip
my hands into it

It grew from nothing
Inside me it grew
It grew in my veins and arteries
   In my bones and flesh
It mastered my blood
One day I found it curled up
   In my skull
Under my useless tongue
Now I have nothing to say
   To anyone

Ladies and gentlemen, all the important signs point to one thing:
          I am a fool
To begin with I got myself born into the wrong class
          and to the wrong parents
With my habits and inclinations I should have contrived to get
          myself dropped on a gold-threaded featherbed
And have selected for my father someone who was not
          a mystagogue but a munitions-maker
My mother was okay but she should have been my father
I've nothing against my brothers and sisters except that they were
          older and had more meat and muscle on their bones
It took me a long time to make out that my teachers
          were ball-less serfs in conspiracy with the Devil
          against intelligence and vitality
That when the strong spoke of law & order they meant
          legalized brigandage
That the weak speak of justice but mean revenge
That civilization is a *pissoir* with paintings by Rubens and Picasso
          on the walls: organ music by Handel and Bach
That not being handicapped in the least by vision or creativity,
          women are by far the stronger sex
That when they speak of love and romance they mean babies
          with hubby pinch-hitting for a baby rattle
That priests and rabbis have every good reason to believe
          in religion: it pays the rent
That poets are talented sickies to be avoided as one avoids
          the adder's bite
It took me too long to perceive that there is a God who doesn't exist
          anywhere, not in the heavens or in the hearts of men
That he reveals himself to the picked few only when he feels
          an uncontrollable desire to hear his own voice
          in the immense solitudes he has created for himself

And speaks to them only to comfort himself through the ineffable
   sound of his voice and to detect whether there has been any
   deterioration in its timbre through the centuries and ages
That I, Israel, can plainly hear his majestic vocables dripping from
   copse and corpse and the flash of a fish
Though I may never hope to make out what he is saying or why he
   prefers to say it the way he does
And that sunlight on leaves and water is his reassuring smile
It has taken me all these years to discover that everything except
   writing poems and making love ends up by finally boring me

BODHIDHARMA

From what sputtering taper
was my light kindled
. . . to sputter in its turn

Detached iotas of flame
fall into the Vast Emptiness
to turn up fragments of poems
floating on its nearest facet.
I roar with furious laughter.

My pleasure in discomfiting
enemies and friends alike
is a gift from the Gautama himself.

And where I turn
I meet myself
striding the other way.

At sudden moments
power can come flooding in
from unseen major stars, from geese
and leaping goats
to soak all my follicles
in the sweetness of Buddhi.

That's why my face
looks like a clenched fist
and I am always irascible.

THE SHARK

In some quiet bay
or deserted inlet
he is waiting for me

It is noon
there is a stillness on water and land
as if some primal god is about to speak;
in the sky
not a single bird is to be seen flying

I shall swim out towards him
bringing him my incurable moral ache
and my cancered liver,
memories of women laughter Greek islands
griefs and humiliations I could find no words for

I want him to be black, wholly black
I want him to be famished and solitary
I want him to be quietly ready for me
as if he were the angel of death

The last thing I want my alive eyes
to behold before I close them forever
are his ripsaw teeth.

Why without cease do I think of a bold youth
    national origin unimportant or racial Peruvian
Russian Irish Javanese he has fine clear eyes
honest smiling mouth a pat for a child's head
talks to old women and helps them cross the street
    is friendly with mainliners anarchs and nuns
Côte St. Luc housewives their ruined husbands and brats
optometrists sign-painters lumpenproletarians dumping
their humps into coffee cups plotting revenge
and clerics who've made out of Christ a bearded faggot

From the rotating movement of a girl's beautiful
    buttocks he draws energy as from the sun
(O lovely revolving suns on Ste. Catherine Street)
and from breasts and perfumed shoulders and hair
Piccadilly Wilhelmstrasse Fifth Avenue rue St. Germain
    the suns go rolling on luminous hoops pinwheels
handsprings and somersaults of desirable flesh
the bold youth with wide-apart happy eyes
stepping lightly over blossoming asphalt graves is running
after them touching a child's head smiling to old women

Why don't I ever meet him face to face?
    sometimes I've seen him stepping off a bus
but when I've caught up with him he's changed
into a bourgeois giving the two-fingered peace sign
or a poet shouting love as if it were a bomb
    on damp days into an office clerk smelling of papers
is he somebody's *doppelgänger*? an emanation or
shadow I see taking shape near a plateglass window?
who is he? he haunts me like an embedded absence
and as if I had lived all my life in arrears

My young son asks me:
"Who's the greatest poet?"
Without any fuss I say, "Shakespeare."
"Is he greater than you?"
I ho-ho around that one
and finally give a hard "Yes."
"Will you ever be greater
than . . . (a splatter of lisped S's
and P's) . . .?"
I look up at my son
from the page I'm writing on:
he too wants his answer
about the greatness of Shakespeare
though only six and carefree;
and I see with an amused hurt
how my son has begun to take on
one of those damned eternal fixtures
of the human imagination
like "God" or "Death" or "the start
of the world"; along with these
it'll be with him the rest
of his life like the birthmark
on his right buttock; so as though
I were explaining God or Death
I say firmly without a trace
of ho-ho in my voice: "No, I'll never
be greater than William Shakespeare,
the world's greatest poetic genius
that ever will be or ever wuz"
hoping my fair-minded admission
won't immediately blot out
the my-father-can-lick-anyone image

in his happy ignorant mind
and take the shine away
that's presently all around my head.
That unclimbable mountain, I rage;
that forever unapproachable star
pulsing its eternal beams from a far
stillness onto our narrow screens
set up as Palomar libraries and schools
to catch the faintest throb of light.
Damn that unscalable pinnacle
of excellence mocking our inevitable
inferiority and failure
like an obscene finger; a loud curse
on the jeering "beep-beeps"
that come from dark silence
and outer galactic space to unscramble
into the resonant signature of
"Full many a glorious morning" or
"The quality of mercy is not strained"
or "Out, out, brief candle. . . ."
NO poet for all time, NO poet
till this planet crack into black night
and racking whirlwinds EVER
to be as great as William Shakespeare?
My God, what a calamitous burden
far worse than any horla or incubus:
a tyrant forever beyond the relief
of bullet or pointed steel. . . .
What a terrible lion in one's path!
What a monumental stone
in the constrictive runnel of anyone
with an itch to write great poems
– and poets so cursed beyond all
by vanity, so loused up in each inch
of their angry, comfortless skin

with the intolerable twitch of envy!
Well, there's nothing to be done
about that bastard's unsurpassable
greatness; one accepts it like cancer
or old age, as something that one
must live with, hoping it will prod us on
to alertest dodges of invention
and circumvention, like the brave spider
who weaves his frail home in the teeth
of the lousiest storm and catches
the morning sun's approving smile;
Anyhow there's one saving grace:
that forever smiling damned bastard,
villain, what-have-you, is dead
and no latest success of his
can embitter our days with envy,
paralyze us into temporary impotency,
despair rotting our guts and liver;
yes, though the greatest that ever wuz
or ever will be he's dead, dead,
and all the numerous flattering busts
keep him safely nailed down
among the worms he so often went raving
on about when his great heart burst
and all the griefs of the world
came flooding out. His ghost may wander
like Caesar's into my tent
by this rented lake, and I'll entertain
him; but he must also stand outside
begging for entry when I keep his volume
shut, and then he's out in the cold
like his own poor Lear. And – well –
there's my six-year-old son
who says of the clothes flapping
on the clotheslines: "Look, they're

scratching themselves," or compares
his mother's nipples to drain-plugs
he says he wishes to pull out, or
tells me the rain is air crying
– and he only four at the time;
and though I swear I never told him
of Prospero and his great magic
asked me the other day: "Is the world real?"
So who really can tell, maybe one day
one of my clan will make it
and there'll be another cock-of-the-walk,
another king-of-the-castle; anyway
we've got our bid in, Old Bard.

When my old schoolfellow
from Baron Byng
went into the insurance game
naturally I let him sell me
an insurance policy

Afterwards it was the furniture
business
and he persuaded me
I shouldn't live another hour
without an armchair
made from the finest imitation leather

Opening a men's haberdashery
for a while he had me
the best-dressed poet
in the world

Then switching to cars
of course he sold me
the most expensive Jaguar
on the lot

Last week when he bought into
a funeral parlour
I decided the time had come
to put an ocean between us

The enormous arch was covered by intricate
designs of great beauty, murals and whole stanzas
of poetry; in between precious stones
glinted or shone like many-hued fires in the sun.
Before passing under the arch everyone gazed
at the magnificent designs and inscriptions,
some for a long time; others stood off at a distance
copying them into books or making careful notes
in the reverential stillness that wrapped them round.
Nature itself seemed bowed in homage, in awe.
Then an odd thing took place before my eyes. I saw
the arch begin to sink into the yielding ground;
at first slowly, then with gathering energy
until by noon tall persons had to bend their heads
before they could pass comfortably through the arch.
At dusk even those who were of medium tallness
had to crouch quite low until it seemed they were
on hands and knees, their backs scraping the grey stones.
Nevertheless many rapt individuals still looked
for a long time and adoringly at the designs
before they walked under the arch though the number
copying or making notes appeared greatly diminished.
The next morning I rose up very early
to see what had become of the fabulous arch.
Even from a distance away I could discern
it had sunk yet more deeply into the soft ground
so that only persons who were very short
could now pass beneath it and even they only after
much straining and discomfort and angry shoves;
within an hour no one but dwarfs, midgets, and runts
and those who trod on stumps, their legs having been sawed
off at the knees, might pass safely through. Nobody

cared any longer to look at the lovely designs
and the adoring copyists had all vanished
– who knows where? I observed the fires from the stones,
precious and many-hued, now slanted above
the foreheads of the straining manikins and cripples
or if by chance catching their eyes made them blink or tear.
By nightfall the dark hordes swollen and thickened
could be squeezed through only by pressing them
so tightly no space was left between body
and body, while some of the beefier dwarfs and shrimps
wearing special armbands and huge orange buttons
would lunge at them as if they were a plastic ball
that could be pummelled into the demanded shape.
So: jostled, shoved, prodded by many blows and swats,
kicked, thumped, slapped, the fused mass of cripples and gnomes
groaning and sweating were propelled under the arch.
The following noon from the high hill where I stood,
the anonymous pressed mass, hot and sticky
under the unmerciful midday sun
and impelled by howling runts in grey uniforms,
seemed to be tar a tar-machine was spurting out
between the stumpy columns to make a fresh road
that stretched bubbling and black farther than eye could see.
Scarcely above it, now full of pocked holes
where once precious jewels had shone and loosed their fires,
the wan and broken span looked like a fading grin.

They supplicate, they pray, their death-like silence
harangues; but chiefly they mock our presence
with their own and mock with such diverse nuance
of malice horror disdain that the prayed-to God
who made and put them here to stand stuffed with straw
withering against the walls or to crouch in glass tombs
surely is abashed, and drowns out with laughter
of his own the savage laughter in these corridors

Look, my friend, at those niches; there you will find
clearly defined what the anthropoid's uniqueness
comes down to: it is to wear grinning at the end
when the years have thwacked and squeezed out all offence
just such a subtle look of meekness and contempt
on your petrified skull. O peerlessly human
is the malediction on those lipless jaws
giving final judgement on our journey here

They mock themselves, they mock their past lives
what they were and what they did: senator
priest physician lawyer and grand lady born
white-gloved and bonneted for the season's ball;
you could say featured here for all to see
is the Christian's venom against the valour
and pride of life and that some rancorous monk
lined up this masque of smirks to mime his fury

Only the children cuddle like faded dolls
left on shelf or wall after the Xmas sale;
they alone lack the look of spiteful mimicry
and present a sad mien, an animal dumbness;
to the women death, it seems, was a trespass

or indignity, perhaps an irksome shift
from a good gossip, a winning game of cards
but the tots, alas, died before they got the drift

All these sad corpses, each one decomposing
in the slow fire of time; on the straw-filled scarecrows
faded cards giving the name and date of expiry
which translates into: "Lord, we have seen the glory!"
Did life pummel them into these grimaces?
Doubtless. My mind caresses each fleering chalky skull
even as it consigns with matching derision
this grisly harlequinade to a blazing furnace

PARQUE DE MONTJUICH

I

In European cemeteries my brothers lie
neither ignored nor neglected; they cause
not even a tremor of shame or embarrassment
but if sometimes thought of, thought of then
as something heteroclite – even intriguing –
like a freakish trinket whose origin has been forgotten

How clean-smelling, how green and fertile
this park, once a Jewish cemetery
where they hauled in the broken bones from the nearby ghetto;
one wonders, standing beside these shrubs, these trees,
did the grass come up cleaner, darker
for marrow and flesh being occasionally toasted?

Yet, look! Beyond the tourist museums Columbus,
in his molten arms the blood of Marranos,
proudly turns his back on the cathedrals and whores;
standing high above the city on his astrolabe
he points his raised finger to the New World
beyond these foul streets, the polluted stinking harbours

II

Prickly as the Jews whose dust they cover
these grotesque misshapen cacti
climb the hot and dusty mountainsides

They cluster in green squalid ghettos
contorting like Hebrew letters some hand dispersed
upon his arid, inhospitable ground

Between them, catching at once mind and eye
the vivid perennial blood-drops of geraniums
that thrive, their stems cut again and again

While towering above red flowers, cacti and rock
brood the dark rabbinical cypresses
giving coolth and dignity to their anguished flock

III

I sit on the weatherbeaten bench. Before me
the busy harbour; yet all that I can see
are the round-roofed steel sheds and cranes
between stone pillars making a perfect
focus for my dazzled eyes. They select
the sheer lines rising grey and plain
though tilting all ways starkly
as if in abstract collusion with the cacti
my gaze takes in on either side
each time I turn my marvelling head

Yet here where each bloom is green or red
where botanists might feel wholly glad
to touch exotic shrubs, flowers, towering palmtrees
I see clearly framed between those pillars now
the black phylactery box on my father's brow
blotting out nature's joyful variety;
smell below these neatly parterred stones
the detritus of long-forgotten flesh and bones
and hear all morning no other sound
but Rachel's voice rising from the ground

MONTJUICH: The old *Montes Judaicus*, i.e., "Jewish Mountain." It was here
that the Jews of Barcelona had their burial ground. Now it is an elegantly
laid-out park overlooking the harbour and the old part of the city.

CABALIST

Always his eyes radiated light;
His gentle voice stirred love and hope.
God was a Presence he could touch,
The mental source of an inner might.
For all that, witless humans seized him
And changed him into a bar of soap.

MIDSUMMER'S DREAM
IN THE VIENNA STADTPARK

Auschwitz, as we know, is on the moon
And Belsen on Mars or Venus.
How can I not believe it?
The waltz strains are so entrancing

Anne Frank is alive and well
And so's her sister Margot;
In fact they're right here in the park
Seated beside the gentleman in the third row.

How handsome the two sisters look
– Anne's eyes, as always, are radiant;
They are drinking in the music
And can scarcely keep their feet from dancing.

And they praise the statue of Johann Strauss,
A single curve of pure delight;
Time sleeps on his violin
And he smiles at them all through the night.

Someone has gone to find their father;
He should be here any minute now.
Ah, happy man, run fast, faster.
Do not stop to wipe your brow.

For all in the park recognize Anne
And stand up as one to applaud her
Because though doomed herself she wept
When she saw gypsy children led to the gas chamber.

FOR 7515–03296

Your eyes are dark and tragic as history
as you stare at the postcard village in the distance;
you are a distinguished graduate from Auschwitz
and mankind's incurable viciousness,
and your slender arm with its tattooed figures
boldly displays your credentials to the world

Each time, my dear, I see your naked loveliness
on this deserted beach my heart is torn apart
by love and loathing, gratitude and disgust,
by reverence and rage until my frantic mind
scurries like that insect between the hot stones
and I grow deaf to all but the waves' savage gulps

And though I know that all the innocent dead
find their resurrection in us and every loving pair;
imaging the dateless horror of the death camp,
the lexicon of human villainy made plain,
I curse without ceasing into the sweet empty air
and feel my loathing for mankind grow as vast as the sea

EUROPE 1976

the lands
east of the Elbe
dark under the Soviet star,
Cimmerian . . .

civilized Europe
finished off for good
by two world wars
Auschwitz and Coca-Cola

decadent, inert
enough energy remaining
only to suffer
evil

and mountains of rich food
to cushion the fall
into nothingness

I am here. The year is haemorrhaging badly.
Nothing can stanch the flow. Go see for yourself
the bloody kerchiefs accumulating in my backyard.
Countless: more flung down every minute
in a comedy of despair. The wind turns up its blast.

Names I give to the reddest leaves dropping
past my window: Hitler, Stalin, Mussolini.
Brilliantly they fared and flared for a season;
now they will lie in a heap, one on top another,
turning to muck in the surrounding ordinary grass.

Dynasties, civilizations flutter past me
in a rain of blood: those that were, those yet to be,
Europe bleeding to death with its murdered Jews. Finis.
The infected brown leaf crimson at the edges has begun to fall.
I listen for the noiseless splash in the immense blood-pool below.

TO THE VICTIMS OF THE HOLOCAUST

Your terrible deaths are forgotten;
no one speaks of them any more.

The novelty of tattooed forearms
wore off quickly; people now say
your deaths are pure invention, a spoof.

More corrosive of human pride
than Copernicus or Darwin, your martyrdoms
must lie entombed in silence.

The devil himself is absolved, polyhistors
naming him the only fascist in Europe
ignorant you were changed into soap and smoke.

That's how the wind blows. Tomorrow
some *goy* will observe you never existed
and the Holocaust your just deserts
for starting wars and revolutions.

I live among the blind, the deaf, and the dumb.
I live among amnesiacs.

My murdered kin
let me be your parched and swollen tongue
uttering the maledictions
bullets and gas silenced on your lips.

Fill, fill my ears with your direst curses.
I shall tongue them, unappeasable shades,
till the sun turns black in the sky.

My son,
don't be a waffling poet;
let each word you write
be direct and honest
like the crack of a gun

Believe an aging poet
of the twentieth century:
neither the Old Testament
nor the New
or the sayings of the Koran
or the Three Baskets of Wisdom
or of the Dhammapada
will ever modify or restrain,
the beastliness of men

Lampshades
were made from the skins
of a people
preaching the gospel of love;
the ovens of Auschwitz and Belsen
are open testimony
to their folly

Despite memorial plaques
of horror and contrition
repentance, my son,
is short-lived

An automatic rifle
endures
a lifetime

FOR MY SONS, MAX AND DAVID

The wandering Jew: the suffering Jew
The despoiled Jew: the beaten Jew
The Jew to burn: the Jew to gas
The Jew to humiliate
The cultured Jew: the sensitized exile
    gentiles with literary ambitions aspire to be
The alienated Jew cultivating his alienation
    like a rare flower: no gentile garden is complete
    without one of these bleeding hibisci
The Jew who sends Christian and Moslem theologians
    back to their seminaries and mosques for new arguments
    on the nature of the Divine Mercy
The Jew, old and sagacious, whom all speak well of:
    when not lusting for his passionate, dark-eyed daughters
The Jew whose helplessness stirs the heart and conscience
    of the Christian like the beggars outside his churches
The Jew who can be justifiably murdered because he is rich
The Jew who can be justifiably murdered because he is poor
The Jew whose plight engenders profound self-searchings
    in certain philosophical gentlemen who cherish him
    to the degree he inspires their shattering aperçus
    into the quality of modern civilization, their noble
    and eloquent thoughts on scapegoatism and unmerited agony
The Jew who agitates the educated gentile, making him pace
    back and forth in his spacious well-aired library
The Jew who fills the authentic Christian with loathing for himself
    and his fellow Christians
The Jew no one can live with: he has seen too many conquerors
    come and vanish, the destruction of too many empires
The Jew in whose eyes can be read the doom of nations
    even when he averts them in compassion and disgust
The Jew every Christian hates, having shattered his self-esteem
    and planted the seeds of doubt in his soul

The Jew everyone seeks to destroy, having instilled self-division
   in the heathen

Be none of these, my sons
My sons, be none of these
Be gunners in the Israeli Air Force

It is themselves they trust and no one else;
Their fighter planes that screech across the sky,
Real, visible as the glorious sun;
Riflesmoke, gunshine, and rumble of tanks.

Man is a fanged wolf, without compassion
Or ruth: Assyrians, Medes, Greeks, Romans,
And devout pagans in Spain and Russia
– Allah's children, most merciful of all.

Where is the Almighty if murder thrives?
He's dead as mutton and they buried him
Decades ago, covered him with their own
Limp bodies in Belsen and Babi Yar.

Let the strong compose hymns and canticles,
Live with the Lord's radiance in their hard skulls
Or make known his great benevolences;
Stare at the heavens and feel glorified

Or humbled and awestruck buckle their knees:
They are done with him now and forever.
Without a whimper from him they returned,
A sign like an open hand in the sky.

The pillar of fire: their flesh made it;
It burned briefly and died – you all know where.
Now in their own blood they temper the steel,
God being dead and their enemies not.

My father had terrible words for you
– whoreson, bastard, *meshumad*;
and my mother loosed Yiddish curses
on your name and the devil's spawn
on their way to church
that scraped the frosted horsebuns
from the wintry Montreal street
to fling clattering into our passageway

Did you ever hear an angered
Jewish woman curse? Never mind the words:
at the intonations alone, Jesus,
the rusted nails would drop out
from your pierced hands and feet
and scatter to the four ends of earth

Luckless man, at least
that much you were spared

In my family you
were a *mamzer*, a *yoshke pondrick*
and main reason for their affliction and pain.
Even now I see the contemptuous curl
on my gentle father's lips;
my mother's never-ending singsong curses
still ring in my ears more loud
than the bells I heard each Sunday morning,
their clappers darkening the outside air

Priests and nuns
were black blots on the snow
– forbidding birds, crows

Up there
up there beside the Good Old Man
we invented and the lyring angels
do you get the picture, my hapless brother:
deserted daily, hourly
by the Philistines you hoped to save
and the murdering heathens,
your own victimized kin hating and despising
you?
       O crucified poet
your agonized face haunts me
as it did when I was a boy;
I follow your strange figure
through all the crooked passageways
of history, the walls reverberating
with ironic whisperings and cries,
the unending sound of cannonfire
and rending groans, the clatter
of bloodsoaked swords falling
on armour and stone
to lose you finally among your excited brethren
haranguing and haloing them
with your words of love,
your voice gentle as my father's

Not only did a loony whore
from whom earlier
seven devils had rushed out
have a vision of Jesus,
and Simon Cephas the Fickle
misnamed the Rock
who saw him face to face
in Galilee
after the crucifixion,
and James, and Paul

My friends, I speak the truth:
he appeared to me also
one day when I was standing
on the steps of an Anglican church,
and hailing me as if
we'd had the same pock-marked rabbi
on Ste. Elizabeth Street
said, pointing to the closed doors:
"Yisroel, what do those elegant WASPS
in there
say about me?"

I was frightened but I replied,
"That you're the Son of God, Jeshua,
and that you asked to be crucified
in remission for their sins."

"*Mishegoyim*," he muttered aloud
in surprisingly clear Yiddish
and hastily re-mounting his moped

disappeared into the traffic,
leaving me his halo
to twirl around my finger
like a luminous bagel

Brother and fellow poet,
is this what you wanted?

The mutterings of bead-counting hysterics?
The snufflings of joyless misfits and cripples
fearful of death, more fearful of life?
The *misereres* of the doomed dregs
in every large metropolis of the world?
The hosannahs of the conformist hordes
stinking of money and respectability?

Is this what you wanted:
the grey suburban church and the greyer people
shambling into it each Sunday
you who openly consorted with whores and drunkards
and so loved laughter and joy
that you were willing to be crucified for them?

Arrogantly I cursed the fig tree
the scribes and pharisees,
my eyes flashing with fierce certitude
my voice made confident by rage.

"We are God's children," I shouted
at my simple hearers
and won them over with bribes of loaves and fishes
a spate of dazzling miracles.

The dead talked, the palsied walked;
the circumcised, their ringlets shaking, roared
each time I tripped up rabbi and sage:
my smile was passed around by my disciples.

"You who are sinless, hurl the first stone!"
My own tongue had formed those words,
my own sweet self, wiser than Gamaliel's.
My frame shook with the thought of my uniqueness.

And perceiving the pride I loathed uncoil itself
I stomped on its grinning mouth; only to see the viper
flee from my heel, swift with my own triumphant cry:
There was no breakout from the imprisoning self.

Till my enemies seized me one terrible night
and bound me fast and dying to a cross.
Then godlike with bitter self-knowledge and sinless
only with my last groan did I give up my pride.

Only for one sickening moment
the houses and the hills of Jerusalem
blur into a pain dull as nausea,
clearing into steel-sharp agonizing focus
as he feels the wet corroding salt
leak down his death-pale cheeks and beard
and his dying senses track the guiltless insect
making a noisome halo around his head

Past houses, past barren outlying hill
there's nothing for his eyes to see . . . nothing;
and nothing is in the red folds of the sky,
no Father's voice to call or comfort him
though they've raised him high enough to hear it:
only the demented noise of the insect
and below that, the Roman soldiers
dicing loudly for his mud-bespattered garments

Though no one has forsaken him, he is lost;
mistaken and lost, and dying for an absurdity:
for a dream, a fairytale, an illusion.
Still, he's not embittered; though bound, he's free,
free at last from hope and self-deception. . . .
An instant before he gave up his ghost
he'd have wiped the troubling mist from his eyes
but the stranger's hands were nailed fast to the cross

They want to talk about theology
I want to talk about murder

They want to talk about a crucified Jew
I want to talk about six million crucified Jews

They want to talk about heaven and its choiring angels
I want to talk about earth and its vicious bipeds

They tell me they are Jews of the New Testament
hungering for universal peace, freedom, *agape*
I tell them they are secretly in love with death

They tell me, holding up their hymnbooks, they are saved
I tell them they are damned

They tell me they are Christians
I tell them they are Xians, baptized heathens, *goyim*

End of dialogue

Give all your nights
to the study of Talmud

By day practise
shooting from the hip

Jean-Paul, you're wrong: hell's not other people
though wrought by them; and of course for others,
not for themselves. Man, a sick animal,
his disappointments armed with an excuse
– a differing opinion, size of ears –
can mutilate a woman's lovely breast
or split in two a venerable skull.

I read some blacks opened six tourists' throats
and painted the beach pebbles with their gore.
Nowadays it could turn out my neighbour
who attends to his roses every night
and lends me his tools to repair my shed
one leaden hour will be my torturer
to hang me by my thumbs till I am dead.

Sectarians can dream of a green place
that purged through suffering men might enter;
of Hell as a providential staircase
that winds its crooked way up to heaven;
if it's blessedness that the sinner craves
redemption is nigh, and so is God's grace:
one day the trumpets blow and he is saved.

But we've seen the fatal arithmetic
of the Selection make all virtues vain:
the shade is patterned to the lamp and room
though the skin once encased a selfless man,
the soap smells no sweeter for his fragrance.
In our modern hells, accident and chance
save; not goodness, not love or providence.
Today, one guards not one's soul but a spoon.

My animals play. They devour the innards of fish,
then jump, romp, attack the air with their paws
and with fiercest catsnarls, their claws sheathed,
wage mock combats for my Roman pleasure.

But man consumes trophies, ingests the souls
of battered men, the agonies of women and children
to energize his pathetic strut across
the wreathed trapdoor that opens on the grave.

The sinister underside of every culture,
his cruelty is no less an exuberance,
a defiance of evil and unbearable pain:
his elixir of life is the blood of the slain.

No matter whose smile he seeks, Dionysus's or Christ's,
he's never more pitiable and terrifying
than when he clears his throat to crow
over the pulped bones of his imagined foe.

Jerusalem, you will be betrayed again and again:
not by the brave young men who die for you
with military cries on their blue lips
– never by these
                  And never by the scholars
who know each sunken goat-track
that winds somehow into your legend, your great name
and not by those dreamers
                         who looking for the beginnings
of your strange wizardry ascend from storied darkness
holding dust and warped harps in their blistered hands

These will always find you and bring you
offerings of blood and bone
                     lowering their grave eyes
as to an idol made neither of wood nor stone
nor brick nor any metal
                yet clearly visible
as though sitting on a jewelled throne

                    O Jerusalem
you are too pure and break men's hearts
you are a dream of prophets, not for our clay,
and drive men mad by your promised
impossible peace, your harrowing oracles of love;
and how may we walk upon this earth
          with forceful human stir
unless we adore you and betray?

SYNAGOGUE IN WEST PALM BEACH

Too elegant, too white, too spacious.

I halt, embarrassed, on the wide boulevard
down which Caesar's legions might march
or a duke's retinue with swords and halberds.
It should be dark and smoky
like God's word,
foreboding and rueful as the eyes of my father,
twisted like crushed limbs.
What, will the Almighty
descend these broad steps in sneakers,
wearing a Panama hat?
Will his voice be a soft breeze
stirring the palmleaves above his house?
Will a limousine stop for him
while his man runs to take the tablets
from his hands?
Will he smile to me in greeting,
displaying perfect manners and teeth?

I miss the smell of onions and piety
and of ancient gaberdines
that shone like boyhood rinks at twilight.
The black-bearded fanatics
whose long bony fingers
hobbled after me like arthritic Hebrew letters
to nightmare my sleep.
The ecstatic cries only torment could reproduce.
Where are the prayers that resounded like curses?
The yellow-black stumps in the beseeching mouths?

Who are those sleek impostors with coiffured heads
and upright backs?

You are mistaken, he said,
I am neither lecher nor womanizer.
If I'm crazy about women
it's for the beauty
some pitying devil threw over them,
a beauty that blinds my gaze to everything
except lips eyes breasts
and roils my blood
like a delicious venom.

When the fit is on me
I am their slave, their man Friday;
they can do with me as they will
and to their absurdest wish
I am as malleable as putty,
more pliant than straw.
For their ally is not beauty alone
but the scantness of sense or purpose
I find in the remotest curved niche
of the universe;
whoever framed its empty immensities
didn't reckon on a man's reason or conscience
or the unassuageable ache in my heart.

Women and poems are my sole chance here
to give expelled breath shape and contour
and fable it with meaning.
I place on the brow of every woman I love
a crown made from the choicest words;
I dress her like a woodland queen
in trope and metaphor.
My desperation blossoms into garlands

braceleting her wrists, my sick despair
into flowering anklets.

I plug the void with my phallus
and making love on bed or carpet
we transfigure pitchblack nothingness
into a puma whose whiskers
we stroke between enrapturing kisses.

Thoughtless and primitive and selling
their woven blankets, these riant blacks
need your maunderings, O shade of Yeats,
like a hole in the head. Your fussy dialogues
smelling of lamp and planed for eternity
seem the self-indulgent fantasies here
of an unexercised man with a weight problem.
I see you climbing your famed tower
out of breath from years and tired lungs,
assaying the pros and cons
of Art and Life, Action and Thought,
and chipping neatly into place as you mount
the lines of your favourite puppets,
Soul and Body, Soldier and Poet,
and all the other brainy dialecticians
you shelter in your vellum pages.

As your portentous shade ascends
Thoor Ballylee, these excitable skinny Caribs
common and noisy in a marketplace reeking
of island spices and human sweat shout, sing
and show their strong white teeth;
insensible of your cultivated worries
or that you, Senator,
Poet, Playwright, Nobel laureate
and Lady Gregory's liveried patrician,
after many subtle nictitations
at Art, the tinted mists of Byzantium
finally avouched your fealty to life.

To life as it's lived by men and women
coupling like toads in cemetery and ditch

or exercising their lithe beautiful bodies
on the soft white sands of their beaches:
beside royal palms and cow tamarinds
living always close to their instinctual wants,
the omniscience in their blood and loins
without your say-so or counsel, O blanched European,
so laden with self-doubts and Irish mists.

At this hour
the figs
look like the tight green testicles
of a youth

Next month
they'll hang loose and furrowed
like an old man's

NARCISSUS

Under a false sky, the raw cloudblots
indecipherable, white and turning grey,
he opens his pores to the indifferent sunshine
and, hostile, smiles at innocent strangers
he secretly wishes at the pool's bottom,
their drowned faces swooning on the surface

Aloof and solitary in his immense perfection
he leaks his image into the elements
and beholds it free of blemish,
without the ravages of guilt and lust,
a pearl flawless in a setting of washed-up faces

Whoever now sees him kneel in adoration
sees a man healed of pain and vileness,
each ripple extending his triumphant leer

O darkening nymphs and satyrs, it's not beauty
transfixes him but Echo who mocks and calls him
a confused ape, a discarded hypothesis

1

God's black angels
can't help alighting
on my arms and shoulders
and irritating the life
out of me
when I'm trying to take
an afternoon snooze

I can't help
squashing the life
out of them
and smearing their pasty guts
on the walls

2

On the flypaper
they look peaceful
as if they'd been
suddenly overwhelmed
by the sweetness of life,
not at all
like the grimacing corpses
in the *Catacombe dei Cappuccini*
their number and death-like silence
remind me of

3

The pale yellow strip
studded with their
black stiffened bodies
and swaying in the gentle
morning breeze
is not without a certain
kind of beauty,
like my mother's cursings
preserved in amber
or Baudelaire's
Flowers of Evil

I've seen the grey-haired lyrists come down from the hills;
they think because they howl with eloquence and conviction
the townspeople will forgive their disgraceful sores
and not care how scandalous and odd they look;
how vain their contrite blurtings over booze and women
or the senescent itch for the one true faith.

Not for me sorrowful and inglorious old age
not for me resignation and breastbeating
or reverbing of guilts till one's limbs begin to tremble
and a man's brought to his knees whimpering and ashamed;
not for me if there's a flicker of life still left
and I can laugh at the gods and curse and shake my fist.

Rather than howl and yowl like an ailing cat
on wet or freezing nights or mumble thin pieties
over a crucifix like some poor forsaken codger
in a rented room, I'll let the darkness come only when I
an angry and unforgiving old man yank the cloth of heaven
and the moon and all the stars come crashing down.

NIGHT MUSIC

I'm in the darkening courtyard
surrounded by a jungle
of flowers ferns and leaves;
above the gloom and leaf-spaces
the stars appear and disappear
like spectral moths caught in a net.
Far below the sea is wearing away rock and stone;
the hilltop castle is crumbling under the moon.

The small stray kitten I plucked
this morning from the cobblestones
is asleep in the hollow
between my knees. She purrs gently,
indifferent to Beethoven's *Kreutzer Sonata,*
or yawns to show me her pink mouth and lips.
Only an occasional puff stirs
fern and leaf and flower,
the shadows they make on the terraced floor.

The music ravishes my ears, stirs
my heart and brain till I become
the blackness and silence that enclose me.
A sudden wind separates the black leafage
above my head, letting me glimpse
the bacterial smear in the sky.
The courtyard is full of small noises
as if Beethoven's notes were scattered
and scampering joyously over petal and fern.

The kitten purrs. Leaves and shadows stir
languorously. In my eyes are uncontrollable tears
for the frustration and futility
in each man's lot, the inadequacies
and confusions which are the burden
and *leitmotiv* of the whole symphony.
No man so deaf that he can't hear it.
For me, from this night on, all's changed.
I have hatched an asp that delays its bite:
there remains only to be desperate and brave.

Pablo Neruda, let me make peace with you.
I have scorned you long enough.
All morning I've read your "Song of Protest"
and been moved to tears and outrage.
Great stuff! Great rhetoric
about South American dictators
and Yankee imperialism though
quaint in places like Shelley's rant
about kings and tyrants
and lacking the complexity of truth.
Still, your loud booming voice
is organ music in my ears
and tolls the death-knell
for navel-gazing poetlings
and broken-in literati
lining up for their uniforms
or jiggling their feminine haunches
for prizes and grants.
Deafen them, Pablo, deafen them!
Make their eardrums bleed
and like a great wind
let your voice tear
the delicate sheets from their hands
and if ghosts have need of bumpaper
give one to that sad singer, Vallejo,
and to the passionate flame that was Machado.

Pablo, I can't help liking someone
who gets excited about injustice and ass,
who makes clever feints against Death
and asks everyone to admire
his deft trickery and showmanship.

You're a poet with panache
and the ladies must have adored you.
But where was your shit-detector
when it came to Stalin
and his evil-smelling crew?
His bloodied hands stank to heaven
yet you took the stink into your lungs
and didn't cough once. Or retch.
Why? Did the Georgian smile
on that human shitpile
fool you? Or his moustache
a wiser poet than you
likened to a cockroach?
By all means one should fight for the poor:
let them have justice and bread
but one should fight without illusions,
without laughing gas in one's cavities.
Do you really suppose the prole
any less envious or vain or cruel
than the capitalist who exploits him?
Or the crushed peasant
any less unjust and vindictive
than the landowner who arrogantly
gallops his steed over him?

I hate all Caudillos
to the right of me and to the left
and I would despatch Castro
with the same equanimity
I'd end the misrule of Pinochet;
I'd send them both, Pablo,
to the same hot crater in Hell.
Since I knew shameful poverty
and exploitation, unlike you
who only read about them in books,

I expect no mortal
to remain decent and sensible
with absolute power in his hands
and know only too well the appetites
that move the rabble in the metropoles,
my awareness of the *condition humaine*
and what humans can do to other humans
taking sleep from my eyes
though every sleepless night
I tell myself the other galaxies
are bursting at the seams with utopias
where fellowship and love
are as plentiful as ass in a bordello
and only your poems and mine, Pablo,
are on the sweet lips of everyone.

His maintenance is human blood;
mine, luckily, is eel and lamb's kidney,
the succulent livers of young chickens.
Nevertheless, his bigoted taste in food
points me to my appointed place
in Nature's vampyric banquet
whose holiness and justice only
my morbid sentience spoils and poisons.

If your mind isn't stuffed with hamburger
and dills, his crimsoned incisors
and thick blackness make clear
before he turns bat or escaping wolf
how under dying suns life and death
are both equally a pain in the neck,
a wound from which there's no recovery:
we must kill one another and die.

This century's agnostic Faust,
he parleys neither with Devil nor God;
nothing comforts him for love's transiency
or beauty's, their ordered come and go. O
his captived soul yearns for immortality
and defying Everyman's sentence of doom,
heroically he opens his sooty wings
above green mud, the incredible haunting snow.

THE SLAUGHTERHOUSE

In the absurd slaughterhouse
that is history
where there are no heroes
but only butchers and slain,
no matter what fables
silly poets tell
and theologians believe,
make certain
the cleaver is yours
and the bared throat someone else's.
But best if, from a safe niche
away from the roar
of those whom power maddens,
you can observe the flashing blades
and the beautiful rosettes
their spilled blood
makes on page and floor

Their shining knives
are poised
            for each other's
throats

Why should I
dance
        between
and deflect their aim?

You stand dumb and tall, Dante.
Even your famed eagle schnozz
is dripping pigeonshit.

Uncaring of your pain and exile
the teachered schoolchildren
turn barnyard fowls, cackle.

Or hoot like young owls
when the taller boys, snickering loudly,
read the eternal commedias
scratched on your pedestal:

"*Ti amo, Ettore*"

Flora
4–0–81
Español

It is the agony of an expiring
Achilles or Lear
my son watches happening
on the white saucer
– his private Globe theatre

Or it's opera:
to the rising blare of its own wings
the stricken fly
storms and lurches
across the brightly prepared stage
like an outraged protesting
Rigoletto

"This one has had it," he says tenderly
when La Mouche rubs her delicate legs
to commence her frantic dance of death;
and feeling a surge of power
he broods over her ineluctable doom
as she goes into her last breathtaking spin

(O tragic joy
that softens eyes and mouth)

Hour after hour
my youngest son watches
the poor ignorant migs alighting
on the poisonous red square
and cannot have enough
of the subtlest elation
known to man

When young
I would shape carefully
                    my grief
if a friend died
or an old bookseller
I loved and admired
                    a dear aunt or cousin

I would gather
                    my tears
into an urn
or channel them
                    with honouring decorum
into elegies and songs
for the dark majestical cypresses
to iterate
                    above sunlit Mediterranean graves

Now
        myself white-haired
and walking steadily
                    into the mist
when someone dies
whom I knew way back
        a schoolfellow from Baron Byng
or the corner groceryman
                    Pentelis Trogadis

I howl like a child
his finger
            jammed
in the doorway

Senile, my sister sings. She sings
the same snatch of song over and over
in a quivering voice, her lips trembling
when she tries for the high notes. Her white
hair close-cropped like a prisoner's
and her unobstructed tongue lolling
over her furrowed lip while her dentures
grin at us through a glass of water,
my sister is some kind of vocal chicken,
especially when her small raisin eyes dart
from visitor to visitor as though about
to pluck worms out of their garments.
My heart breaks, remembering her beauty
and wit, the full mouth with a tale in it
she finally exploded in our ears.
Is this my sister so frail and emaciated,
whose valour and go were family legends,
her smiles so dazzling they made the roaches
leisurely roaming the walls of our kitchen
scurry behind the torn wallpaper
to hide there till the incandescence had passed?
Sing, my dear sister, sing
though your trembling lips break my heart
and I turn away from you to sob
and let the tears course down my cheeks,
my grief held back by pride and even a kind
of exultance. You do not moan or whimper,
you do not grovel before the Holy Butcher
and beg Him to spare you days; or rock
silently like the other white-haired biddies
waiting to be plucked from their stoops. No,
though His emissary ominously flaps his wings

to enfold you in their darkness, you sing.
Your high-pitched notes must rile him
more than rage or defiance. You sing him
no welcome, and if your voice trembles
it's not fear or resignation he hears
but the cracked voice of the *élan vital*
whose loudest chorister you are, abashing Death
and making him skulk in his own shadow

THE GARBURETOR

How, I wonder, did Frost and Yeats
pull it off? I mean
how did those two old sods
manage to play the bard,
to look so solid and respectable
while stuffing their built-in garburetors
with the rubbish of daily living?
Weren't their noses, just once,
pulled out of joint? Didn't tears start
in their eyes from the lousy smell?
Didn't they ever pass a mirror
on the way to the dais or platform
to give a reading
and observe how ridiculous they look,
how loosely their clothes
hang on their indecent selves?

I can't be sure of my feelings
from one hour to the next;
each day I murder a different
relation or friend, uncertain
from what quarter
honour or betrayal will come.
In my mind heroes and villains
keep changing places
and the only thing I know for sure
is that I want to throw a bomb
on the Kremlin
and string Castro up by his balls:
there's the needle points me to sanity!
Apart from all that, all options are open
and my mind masticating radiant czarinas

stars, goldfish, and dynasties is an ant
scurrying around for the carcass
he's dropped somewhere on the sand.

Sure, the poems are something else;
solid and packed tight,
the pain and lies bleached out of them
or transfigured to look like Truth
and always, of course, Beauty.
They fool most of the people most of the time;
even fool the demented fool who's packed them
so that he reads them without a quaver
of misgiving or self-doubt,
the eternal debates temporarily ended
the antinomies that plague him stilled
and the whirring of the garburetor
silenced just long enough
to let him hear the deafening applause.

The ant skitters
on the bricked terrace,
all its movements
random and unpredictable
as the first two lines of a poem

Until it encounters
the detached wing of a fly
and stops abruptly
to see what it is
and what he must do about it

After that the lyric unfolds
more slowly, its bearing sealed
by the accident of the fly's wing
and generating phrase
by phrase its own terrace

I put down my book
   and stare at the distant haze;
the loud-voiced Greeks around me
   chomping on their fish and *peponi*
must reckon I'm having age-old thoughts
   on the human condition.
Noisy fools. I'm thinking of the waves
   gently cupping the breasts
of the lovely nymph just risen from the sea
   and the water lapping
her thighs and her delicate love-cleft

When she swims away
   she pulls my thoughts after her
in watery streaks of light. I become
   the sea around her
and she nestles in my long green arms
   or is held in the flowing
wavelets of my white hair. I billow
   above her like a dolphin
stroke her limbs and nip her rosy neck and shoulders
   with sharp unceasing kisses
till languorously she slips to the ribbed sand
   where under the haloing starfish
fern weed and enamoured seasnake I quiver
   between her silver thighs

L'ENVOI

If this were the last
absolutely the last
                    poem
you were ever going to write,
what would you write?

"World, you old smelly cunt
it's been great knowing you;
knowing sun, moon, stars, beautiful women
waves and graves

I leave you now
for one that has no smell
                    a Greek urn
Good-night, and farewell"

THE ANNUNCIATION

What angels will we meet on the way to the post office?
What kisses will the leaves rain down on your neck?
Your footsteps leave no shadows on the ground
for the morning sun makes a bale of them
which he tosses over the first white fence that we pass

The announcing angel robes himself in ordinary dress.
What name does he whisper in your perfumed
and delicate ear? Judith? Deborah? Eve?
When you incline your fragrant head to listen,
the storewindows blaze and shine and the village street

Robed in its summer foliage resounds like a West Point
salute with the sound of uncorked champagne bottles;
all the birds in the street take the noise
for cues and suddenly whole orchestras of them
and the singing choirs of girls and boys

Make such a jubilation, it frightens off
all evils and sorrows forever; your burgeoning form
parts the air before us like a sorcerer's wand
and the angel in ordinary dress extricates a wing
and blesses its bounty with his own bright feathers

Rum and Coke in my hand,
I blast the cherry pits
two at a time into the grass

My thoughts skimming the air
have the lazy saunter
of a butterfly

Only later
the newsboy's whistle will loose
the day's events, yelping like a pack of dogs

Wherever they are, Camus and Sartre
can aim their halos at each other like Frisbees
or hump the nearest cloud

It's so quiet in the garden
I swear I can hear the insects
clambering over petal and leaf

And I let them track perfect joy
back to my first childhood recognitions
in chokecherries and summer dust

When the dying sun shone forever
and no stalking cat
still as the air around me

Mocked all my loves

My father's name was Moses; his beard was black
and black the eyes that beheld God's light;
they never looked upon me but they saw
a crazy imp dropt somehow from the sky
and then I knew from his holy stare
I had disgraced the Prophets and the Law.

Nor was I my mother's prayer;
she who all day railed at a religious indolence
that kept her man warm under his prayershawl
while her reaching arm froze with each customer
who brought a needed penny to her store;
added to another it paid the food and rent.

An ill-matched pair they were. My father
thought he saw Jehovah everywhere,
entertaining His messengers every day
though visible to him alone in that room,
where making his fastidious cheese
he dreamt of living in Zion at his ease.

My mother: unpoetical as a pot of clay,
with as much mysticism in her as a banker
or a steward; lamenting God's will for her
yet blessing it with each Friday's candles.
But O her sturdy mind has served me well
who see how humans forge with lies their lonely hell.

Alien and bitter the road my forbears knew:
fugitives forever eating unleavened bread
and hated pariahs because of that one Jew
who taught the tenderest Christian how to hate
and harry them to whatever holes they sped.
Times there were the living envied the dead.

Iconoclasts, dreamers, men who stood alone:
Freud and Marx, the great Maimonides
and Spinoza who defied even his own.
In my veins runs their rebellious blood.
I tread with them the selfsame antique road
and seek everywhere the faintest scent of God.

ANARCH

My uneasiness before trees. Nothing
cures me of it or ever will. I'm one
my humanity dooms to gaze at their tall
composed shapes with longing; praying
for bright-wing'd insects to stitch me

By their sallies, their senseless thrusts
into the green palmate leaves I see filtering
the viscous sunshine into a rose decanter
each opened bud this tranquil morning
offers the surrounding thoughtless air

My head's too stuffed with griefs
contemporary and classical to know
beneficence today as any grey trunk proud
of its leafy medallions and fluttering them
like a Soviet commander for all to see

A decaying bug-eyed humanist, I rot
into this murderous century, smiling
tolerantly in all directions, my
blue and gentle eyes beseeching forgiveness
for the compost odours rising like a tide

But sometimes I turn my eyeballs around
to see my skull's interior, become
a mad neurologist and probe with poised lens
the mechanism of brainfold and nerve
that ticks towards the bright disaster

That must one day blot out the heavens,
the agony of innocents caught like a lynx
in the steel trap of human malice
or harpooned like those other Jews,
the harried whales of the prosperous sea.

EINE KLEINE NACHTMUSIK

I was nowhere near
the syphilitic whore called Europe,
smelling of charnel houses and museums

And was not there
when you ripped open the bellies
of pregnant women

Nor when you laughed uproariously
at the spectres
clawing one another for offal

I was not there when you made skeletons
dance for you
and grief-crazed Jewesses to sing

If you're dead
you're beyond my curses and contempt,
inviolable as a jackal's calcified turd

But alive and still insurable,
you're probably in Obersalzberg
letting Mozart ravish your souls

Or in Budapest, Vilna, Cologne
buying sausages, perhaps
Xmas toys for your grandchildren

Why not? Since power's the world's standard
it's your victims, not you,
who feel besmirched and guilty

Ah, *meine Herren*, we live in a time
when atrocity's the norm
and survival the sole merit

In 1980 everyone lives
with some gas in his lungs.
No one will die of it

God made the viper, the shark, the tsetse fly.
He made the hyena, the vulture, the stoat.
By the time He made man
He had the combination down perfect.

How majestic they were
a brief month ago, tall-erect;
now bare but for petals
that reach out like begging hands.

Blind Oedipus and his companion,
they lean against the air
and mock the betraying sun.

The morning glory's faded beauty
is no comfort, nor the white ash of my cigar.
I know what I know. Everything flows;
living, dies: the intruding dog in my garden,
the butterflies cavorting
over the plundered mounds. The white disaster
is on the way
and will not be stopped.

I think of the young Marx,
heaven-storming Promethean, making
kings and capitalists quake
with his *Grundrisse*, his black smouldering eyes
– praising unalienated man, Superman!

"I sowed dragons' teeth and reaped pygmies."

No, my red Messiah, tempestuous Jew.
Your sunflower beauty still flourishes,
astonishes; still rouses man-enslaved man,
poet and mad philosopher
at noonday and in the stillest hour of the night.

Just think, dear girl, the polio virus
owns the same chemical factory
as wisteria or a chimp; as,
when they were alive, Alexander and Darius.

And the fecund infinite variety
you say you reverence in nature,
why, it's that sporting lady
playing the numbers game.

Black holes in space, mice, moons, and fungi,
all move to the same disco beat;
from giant nebulae to mites however small
one unitary law governs them all.

Only my mind arrests that shuttle,
slows down waves to a heave of graves
or keeps a star's sparkle in a verse
till, in a flash, the whole show dissolves!

Fashioned from moisture and dust,
a predator no less than wolf or fox
I nevertheless alight on far-flung galaxies:
temporary icefloes under my mental stride.

Yes, love, there's change, unresting change
in the changeless eternal froth. Yet
haven't you seen how bacteria on dead bodies
shine and make light of death?

Ripe plums are on the table.
I can bang the cupboard door shut.
Eternity dots the kitchen with particulars.

Why should I listen to the impotent whirr
of wings, the buzz-buzz of fat flies,
the sunlight shrunk to what's on their backs?
To a chromatic sneer?

What have I to do with hell's shriekdoms
or the pursy sons of Abraham?
What fly threatens foreclosure
if I don't turn up my hearing-aid?

In my garden the only sounds I hear
are leaves rustling, the receding purr of tires.
The morning glory opens its countenance
to the world. How fresh everything smells.

Remote from all men lie for and kill
I am on holy ground. The innocence
of nature's cannibalism heals and purifies.
The grass's whispering stuns me.

GREETINGS

The black squirrel
in the tree,
jumping from arm to arm
pulls the sunlight after him
before hiding in a cleft
where his long agitated tail
is the day's
golden tongue greeting me

A milkwhite kitten
curled up
    on the bough
of an appletree

A gigantic blossom
until
        its green eyes
blink

What can I know?

Only this mob of leaves
moving with the breeze,
each fragrant puff of air.

Men's despair and malice
covering the earth
like spears of grass.

Or the traffic's roar
beyond my garden
smelling of fresh rain.

The tremulous black-coated squirrel
all instinct and fear,
unique as the tree's bark.

Or that white butterfly
sailing evenly between
warring schools of philosophy.

My own storm-tossed soul,
a troubling joy
since the day I was born.

Finally: the remote sky
from which no conclusions
may ever be drawn.

Into the ordinary day you came,
giving your small nose and chin to the air
and blinded by the noise you could not see.
    Your mother's smile was your benediction;
my wonderment will accompany you
all your days. Dear little girl, what blessings
shall I ask for you? Strong limbs, a mind firm
that looking on this world without dismay
turns furious lust into love's romance?
    These, my child, and more. Grace keep you
queenly and kind, a comfort to the ill and poor,
your presence a bounty of joy to all
that have vision of you, as I have now
who hold your fingers in my trembling hand.

THE GARDEN

Insects display their different shapes
on sunglasses, on table and book;
not one that isn't the slime of time
or doesn't ask from me a wise look.

The butterfly's flutter on a tall stalk
is my heart's beat in space, O gentle
and steady as my best morning thoughts.
I'd paint them or birds were I Chagall.

Give them *yarmulkas* to fly to
and sobbing music from the *shtetl*;
they would flap their crazy wings with joy
and make their certain way to Zion.

How easily, it seems, I might dissolve
into my chair or surrounding air;
become the dirt my feet walk upon,
grow bright flowerets instead of hands.

No more than a dog's bark are we all;
leaf fall or cat's momentary fright
on the retina: here, only to
disappear into the endless night.

The grass is waiting to cover me
like a warm overcoat, green with age;
the bough's luxuriant leaves are sleeves
ready to embrace or hold me down.

Nature conspires with and against
me, brief shuttle between womb and tomb;
a centimetre on which is notched
immense vistas of anguish and gloom.

Confidently I sit here and write
though dark shadows gather near the house
and the birds have left off their singing.
The fly's cry is trapped in the neat web.

One day, my head full of summer noise
or an étude by Frederic Chopin,
the wind lifting me up by the elbows
will hustle me out of the garden.

Other insects shall come, other leaves grow.
This garden will never be empty;
my wraith will be that white butterfly.
Return a thousand years from now and see.

When hourly I praised her perfect mouth
How could I have known, with lust besotted,
That Satan himself had forged those red lips
To singe my wings, to crisp me like a moth?

I lie on my hotel bed
and watch the clouds move across the sky;
they are in no hurry, they move slowly,
but they never pause or rest.
They are light and have their place
   in the universe.
When I close my eyes I can imagine
I have been dreaming of sheep.
The days also pass slowly.
They too are light and have their place.
I swim, converse with a friend, read poetry.
   Everything passes, even a woman's malice
when she knows she is no longer loved
and her body, no longer desired, is only
a heavy insupportable weight to be coddled
   and dragged from room to room,
its orifices useless.
But that woman too has her place in the universe
   and moves relentlessly on.

At the height of their bitter quarrel
the wretched woman taunted him:
"Poetry is one thing, life another."

And indeed she was right to do so,
for her brief days will soon be over
but she will live infamous in his poems forever.

THE BREASTSTROKE

May the gods be praised that I should meet
on my final lap to the eternal sea
one so young, so gracious and lovely,
under clear skies promising as herself.
Ankled deep in the scorching sands
I can hear the shouting tide; in it
invitation and menace like the smile
on the fair face of my companion,
making me wish to nuzzle forever
between her firm thighs and cover
her mouth with long hungering kisses.

Insensate to everything but her warm flesh
I'd float out into the voluptuous sea,
my practised breaststroke perfect at last.
The heaving mounds press against me,
alluring me past the white wavecrests
that close behind like tall portals
barring return. Green towers collapse
on bright medallions larger than suns;
the virginal foam breaks into bridal cries
and after the last loud crash of savaging breasts,
into the long silence that no man hears.

THE WHEEL

By the polluted lake
the terrorized worms keep all their resolutions;
birds fly past my fears,
indifferent to malice or despair
or the book I hold up
to mirror their ecstatic flights.
My stockinged feet might be
stubble rotting back into earth;
the sandals beside them,
dew-wet and modest in the grass
and remaining close to all my contradictions,
those Jeshua wore when he walked on water.
I have divested myself of everything
except some remembered griefs
I roll like spotted dice
which an imaginary hand thrusting
down like water from a spout
scoops up for the return throw.
My friends, it was never my intention
to play games with Time or Fate or Chance
and for certain not with Death
or to scatter foolish words about
in poems and conversation
concerning the weather in my skull.
Who cares how anyone fares
or what devils he exorcises
with a ripe strawberry leaf
or a rusting nail
extracted from an old horseshoe?
If I stretched out on the grass
in mimic sleep or death
the dice would roll over my face,

yet no finger of mine unbend
to arrest the glittering parabolas
brazing dream and reality
or to mute the thunders in my head.
The air would close over me
like water over the demented fish
in the lake,
magnifying the raw welts
which this age
brutal with madmen's fugues
rubs into my back and shoulders;
the tears swollen and cold
from wild unblinking eyes that stare
at the polluted droplets
erasing into bubble and froth
and once again preparing
the loose folds of my naked flesh
for the next relentless turn of the wheel.

I think of Ovid and the merry twinkle
in his eyes as he fingerfucks the dressed-to-kill
matron sitting beside him while her husband
facing them on the opposite side of the table
feelingly descants on Plato's ION
– he's no fool that man, knows a thing or two
about the arts, is even flattered by the famous poet's
attentions to his wife – and the other guests,
a noted critic of plays among them, a Proconsul
just returned from Alexandria and a clutch
of minor poets cutting their envious teeth
on Virgil's shanks but plainly intending Ovid's,
bare their teeth in vinous approbation. The husband
is very obviously pleased with himself
and the unexpected impression he's made on everyone.
His wife is beautiful, the much-sought-after Ovid
is sitting at her side, filling her glass
and paying her compliments that are making
her squirm and giggle with laughter.
It's a scene that would move anyone
always tuned-in like himself to what's significant
and meaningful in this wretched world
and always eager to seize whatever enjoyments
it keeps locked up in its hidden storeroom.
His educated mind calls the live composition
in front of him *Beauty and Fame* but swiftly
changes it round out of deference to Ovid's
greatness. He's touched to discover so much
sensibility in himself, such a quick and lively mind
– true, his host has not been stingy
with his best Falernian and the guests
have been attentive, even flattering

213

to the provincial pair though his good-looking wife
would win the heart of Caesar himself,
the old curmudgeon – and so he lets himself go,
pulls out all the stops and speaks with unwonted
persuasive eloquence and warmth, with real passion
about *poesis*, glancing at the renowned poet
from time to time to see how he's making out,
whether his words have been winged with divine fire.
Meanwhile Ovid all evening has been keeping up
a steady pressure on the proud matron's clit,
stroking it gently, using only one finger
– the experienced lecher – till he feels a gush
of cuntjuice, warm and viscous, suffuse
his finger and run down his wearied hand.
Only now does he smile to the moist-eyed husband
whom emotion has finally choked up. He smiles
approvingly, genially; he smiles from a full heart,
knowing that in an uncertain world
where death and a woman's scheming hypocrisy
are the only things a sensible man will bank on,
and men are black-hearted and joyless,
only the cold lusts of money and position
exciting them, the gods approve an innocent
fingerfuck giving pleasure to himself and the lady
and making her come – decorously as the occasion
required; and that this or the real thing itself
(screw the fine things promised by dictator or sage)
is a mortal good within our mortal means
before we join the joyless shades of Hell.

INSPIRATION

I have brought you to this Greek village
famed for its honey
as others are for their bread or wine
Love-making kept us awake
half the night
afterwards the jiggers took over
and would not let us sleep
Cocks and crowing women
woke us from our troubled doze
We compared laughingly the red bruises
on our arms and cheeks
Your good mouth, as it always does,
made me drool
and my spirit rose at once
In this stupid century
addlepated professors and mechanics
decry Inspiration
Alas, their arms have never held her;
gazing at you, woman,
in this shy early morning light I could more easily
doubt the feel of the bare boards under my feet
Truly this goddess has being
– in you, in some rare almost forgotten poems
and the mountainous hills and sea
which are waiting for us to look at them,
this vinestem curling on our windowsill
this bee
Come, let us show them
the fierce lumps on our divine foreheads

Skyros, Greece,
June 10, 1972

PARTY AT HYDRA
for Marianne

The white cormorants shaped like houses stare down at you.
A Greek Chagall perched them there on the crooked terraces.
The steep ascent is through a labyrinth of narrow streets
Cobbled with huge stones that speak only Arvanitika.
A surfeit of wisdom has made the stars above you eternally silent.
Many are ambushed by the silence and many never find their way
To the house where the perpetual party is going on.
If you are on the lookout for monsters or demons
You will not find their legs sprawled out in the terraces.
They are all assembled at the house threshing one another
With extracts from diaries whose pages fly open releasing beetles
That crawl along the grapevines and disappear into a night of ears.
Though only one head can be seen, several monsters have seven
And some have three and some no more than two. Beware of the one-
Headed monster with an aspirin in his hand who'll devour you instead.
You know the number of heads each has by the small sucking winds
They make as they dissolve the salads and meats on their plates. So
Listen carefully holding a lighted incense stick for a talisman.
A rutting woman lets her smile float on your glass of punch.
You scoop it up to hand back to her on a soaked slice of lemonpeel.
A poet announces to everyone not listening he has begun a new poem.
He hears a spider growling at him from a suntanned cleavage
And at once pierces it with a metaphor using its blood for glue.
A married man discourses tenderly on love and poultices.
It is almost dark when a goddess appears beside you.
She guides your hand under her white robe and murmurs
"The sweat of invalids in medicine bottles is not love
And wisdom is love that has lost one of its testicles.
Desire is love's lubricant yet love is no wheel spinning in a groove.
Love resides neither in the body nor in the soul
But is a volatile element reconciling spirit to flesh.

216

Love is the holy seal of their interpenetration and unity
When they come together in the perfect moment of fusion.
If you wish to know more about love listen to the crickets on the moon
And emulate the silent shining of the stars but do not become one."
When she vanishes your hand is a river you swim in forever.

Great lover, your sweetness is lost forever
thought and discourse being, alas, much tougher
than when you were alive and wrote: but I've seen
your tomb and naked un-English statue, your ass
your bronze ass turned to the sea – I wonder why

I would have had you facing it, staring down
its famous inquietude as a poet should
though listening always to its many voices
nor would I have stuck that ridiculous scroll
in your hand. Rupert, I think the sculptor

Greek no doubt modelled you on the "Discus Thrower"
or "Apollo Belvedere," put in inspired splashes
of both and made your exquisite Saxon head
too small for the classical legs and torso.
The thing's a mess and that's the brazen truth.

Yet though the sun was hot and high over
Skyros I mounted the hill wanting to see
your tomb and statue for a schoolboy once
in Baron Byng I memorized your sonnet which begins
"If I should die think only this of me. . . ."

And this morning in the Hotel Xenia I recited
all of it to my girl over a *portokalada.*
So you're not quite dead though your great fame
will not come back again. No matter poet and lover
of inns and chinaware, of quiet country lanes

Though the brute world in the shape of this gravel truck
has thrust itself under your moulded genital,
quit of phony accent, the mannered phrase, your hang-up
with language and beauty comes through – the poet's
timeless eponym none can fake or erase.

Skyros, Greece,
June 14, 1972

Appetite and chance, luck and desire
together make a man's fate
not the foolish lines on his palm nor the conjugation
of stars in space rule his lot
but these intangible bars infrangibly up and down
on which if he pleases he can graph his days
until he falls from their arching bough
like a ripe fruit to rot or burn

But a man's ball spins merrily merrily
in the roulette wheel of sexuality
at last comes to rest in a gay groove
red black black red fifteen or fifty-one
to the bored indifferent croupier it is all one
scramble your gamble, ramble and gambol
the appointed groove hole slot is always there
waiting for the balls to come tumbling in

Only a few have the guts to shoot themselves
outside where the despair of the casinos
is a sighing fragrance among the leaves and flowers
when the luck has been consistently bad
and all is lost, even that lovely fire
that flamed and flared in thighs and testicles
but at home the defeated roam from room to room
or run from corridors that come running after them

Or hunt for weapons that will let them stay
the sharp remorse-killing knife and loaded gun
to finger lovingly and to put away;
of one dubious luck the poet alone is lord
good or bad let the gods who flay him say:

to find a memorable name for his anguish
a fat phrase for his woe or a rhyme for the crime
when fortune reloads her glass and carefully takes aim

My youth will not come again
let my gaze be that of the sun, a bold eye
in a bright blue sky, a Greek sky and high
high over the riotous men and women who dance
to the clanging tunes of appetite and chance;
other gods for other men, idols or frauds; mine
be only these to the end of my stubborn days
mine be the brave grateful heart to give them praise

She was from Tokyo.
He was from Tabriz.
They met in a bookstore.
They both reached for the same book.
Excuse me, in Japanese.
Excuse me, in Persian.
The book was a treatise on the cockroach.
Each wanted the book.
There was only one copy.
They agreed to purchase it together.
Both were specialists in the make-up
and behaviour of cockroaches.
Fascinated lifelong students they were.
Now they became fascinated with each other.
They fell in love looking at charts of cockroaches
ingesting whatever it is cockroaches ingest.
He took her to his apartment.
She took him to hers.
They went for long walks together.
They frequently talked about other things
besides cockroaches.
He read her his favourite Sanskrit poets.
She read him Haikus.
Examining the reproductive organs of their favourite
insect, their genitals became moist.
In his apartment; then in hers.
It was delightful.
It was romantic.
They were exceedingly happy.
The affair should have lasted forever.
It brought a shine to their eyes.
It did something to their voices.

They were very tender to each other.
He brought her some verses of his own.
She had a gift for him flown in from Tokyo.
Then one day they had a disagreement.
It was over the feeding habits of the cockroach.
He said one thing, she said another.
The disagreement became an argument.
The argument became a quarrel.
The quarrel became violent and bitter.
They could not agree on the feeding habits of the cockroach.
The gulf between them grew wider and wider.
He said this, she said that.
There could be no compromise.
Only one could be right.
They hissed at each other.
Their eyes filled with hatred.
They questioned each other's intelligence and lineage.
All the lovely, meaningful things they had said to each other
about cockroaches were forgotten.
It was sad.
It was very sad.
It ended with his taking his verses back.
She told him to keep the treatise on the cockroach
since plainly he needed it more than she did.
Bitch, in Persian.
Ignorant louse, in Japanese.
So the affair ended.
It was sad.
It was very, very sad.

Awareness of death's pull
into nothingness
begets tyrant and sadist
but the prod, the harsh shove of love
makes the defiant artist
dance on his tightrope

When death
comes for you, my dear,
let him take you
like a candleflame
that is taken
from its wick
by a gentle stir
of wind
smelling of lilac

BRIDEGROOM

Submissively the young camel
kneels before the altar
to receive his cumber

As he raises the load from the ground
his thin lips flutter
with pride and satisfaction

Superciliously
he trots down the church aisle,
his hooves making a soft sound

TWO WOMEN
for Bobby Maslen

Two women I once knew lie in these mounds of silence;
each in her own way was extraordinary.
One, rebel and feminist long before her time,
a Greek George Sand beautiful and defiant
whose distinction won her enemies everywhere,
the natural enemies of the aristocrat.
She took a lover in this Christian village,
loved and was loved while their loathing grew;
the men's out of baffled lust, the women's
because their mirrors showed them commonplace
beside the unfair radiance that was her portion.
Virtue is most often envy at another's grace
and never was so much virtue found in one place
as in this village where prodigal Stella
lived unabashed her turbulent life
till the grim dames changed her to a toothless crone
and sat her mumbling on her unwashed steps,
her legs thick as an elephant's, giving off smells.
Then, as if Jesus had come, envy changed into pity
and stone-hearted rancour into charity
and smiles wreathed all faces where once were frowns
till one morning when all the villagers were at church
the old decrepit iconoclast and rebel
whom so much Christian love had quite unhinged
poured kerosene over her tattered dress
and putting fire to it became the flaming torch
that always lights up for me her imagined face.
Her charred remains are under that stone
and here are my flowers for her unquiet grave.
The other was an American woman
deformed from birth who fled country and kin

fearing looks and derision for the small hump
she carried on her back like a snail's house.
It's difficult for the frail and weak to live
among the strong whom strength makes insensitive
to woes they may imagine but can never know.
Here in this village she lived among the humble
who pitied and loved her as an angel
who'd fallen from the sky and breached her spine
that mending had grown twisted as an olivetree.
And she gave back their love in full, detailing
their lacklustre village lives on canvases
glowing with her genius and affection
though her face never lost the stranger's smile,
the exile's grimace that still twists into my grief:
women washing their clothes, combing their hair,
the children sinister with birds and cats
and the men idling in the *kafénions*
or salting the fish in their wooden frames.
In her slow-paced crab-like walks she saw light
everywhere, filtering it through brush-hair
and acrylic: in the thin sentinel glasses filled
with ouzo, the furrowed faces of the village gossips
and the thick roadside dust on quincetree and vine;
always she proffered an ironic affection to the *pappas*,
their black beards parting the morning sunshine.
That's her grave, not five paces from Stella Ionnou's
and above the Greek inscription which translates
"Death exists only for those who are still alive"
her simple name salutes you. PEGGY SYLVIA

Molibos,
August 17, 1977

There are chameleons, crab spiders
and certain kinds of women

When my angel's with me
she quotes Hegel and Santayana
and scowls darkly as if the Sphinx
had asked her a riddle

When she's with a playboy
from darkest Manhattan or Chicago
she laughs like an idiot
and tells everyone to piss off

If she's talking to an obvious con-man
I'm ready to lay odds
she'll pull enough tricks of her own
to leave him begging his subway fare

And there are the hunting spiders
more ferocious and cunning than tigers;
when they strike they never miss.
Their innocent malevolence fascinates me

Flourishing nature's oriflamme
her gonfalon of hurt
medusas drop from wavecrest and white foam

In cities they wear fawning smiles
speak only to deceive
and possess two eyes
out of which look cruelty and lust

Observe: among them only poets and saints
are kind, having been born cross-eyed

Listen to the feral cries
of the wild-eyed medusas:
I'm a Christian, I'm a Maoist,
fascist, Marxist, nationalist
I believe in progress and the rights of man

Foamblobs
time's ever-ready spike deflates
and smears like the brown scum
on the rocks below my feet

In Greece, jellyfish are called *medusas*.

THE PRIZE

For years he grew them lovingly
and because he was so devoted
to their glory, unfailingly
his entries won him top awards

One afternoon, his garden radiant
as the Garden of Eden,
reaching for his prize-winning rose
he felt the sharp sting of a thorn

The next day he was useless
from his collarbone down
and only with his wife holding him
will he ever walk again

Mr. X ended his final colloquium on the True, the Good
and the Beautiful ten minutes ago; open mouthed, he's
snoring on the bench

Yesterday we cremated the last Nihilist

The Dialectical Materialists are going mad and hanging
themselves

If the Valium doesn't arrive soon I fear the Christians will
cannibalize their only sons

The volumes of theology and metaphysics have become dust traps

Nobody even watches the shadows anymore

Sweetie, plug up the chinks in the wall

It's getting colder and darker

Stoke up the fire and spread around the blankets

Does anyone know any card tricks, or a song?

An anecdote, nothing sad nothing tragic

Or a story with a punchline to crack us all up

We can speak the words, my dear, of forgiveness
but only our actions could have healed us;
now we're both doomed to incompleteness
and to grimace as though with Bell's palsy.
I was just beginning to see through words,
my friend the enemy, the tricks he plays
with false bottoms and sawed-up ladies,
the will-o'-wisps he'd have me take for real;
you, at last, to see me with love's insight,
the compassion that only wisdom gives.
Now we're like the absurd figures of Pompeii
forever arrested in a vague stance,
a gesture never to be completed,
dumb in the stillness our lava's made.
How words have fooled me all these years,
deceived me like the witches on the heath:
yet poor Macbeth was a poet also
and only poets can misconstrue where
the Banquos without a stitch of imagination
see only hideous misshapen hags about
and rightly smell the mess they're cooking.
If a Banquo croaks it's only because
an assassin's prosaic poignard
gets him in the gut; it's never dreams,
or ambition, the mad reaching out for greatness
and distinction, an immortal name
defying old Skull-and-Bones bringing
oblivion in his grinding white molars.
So farewell, my love, a long, long farewell;
maybe the Atlantic will wipe out the guilt,
the knowledge of wrongs done and suffered;
maybe in some other life I'll be asked

to cover the fourth wall of Paradise
and unlike del Sarto not have to choose
betwixt love and art but, blessed, have both.
But in the here and now I have a misery
to last my life and if I don't tear a hole
in my heart as wide and deep as its pain
it's because I've Byron's way of seeing things
and think death even more absurd than life
and once dead there's no more laughing then.

They heiled him when the motorcade raced past.
They shouted and cheered.
Many wept from ecstasy
and sank down on their knees.
Pride swelling their neck muscles,
they raised extended arms
and swore him boundless allegiance.
Now their corpses lie on the frozen earth
in rigid tribute to the cold
or have twisted themselves into black swastikas
littering the white plain
like jimmies on an enormous frosted cake.
Count them if you can. Thousands, tens of thousands:
their mouths still open on a last shout,
their out-thrust jaws blue and defiant.
With glazing eyes some greet
Death's motorcade swirling past
in long grey columns of snow.
This is what they wanted all along.
This is what they came for.
Awesome and grand to watch them sink to the ground
beneath his classic salute.

At dawn, it all becomes visible at once,
some things in sharper detail than others;
only at the edges farthest from the risen sun
there's a greyness like a grey pall of smoke.
This could be Venice and the sky
by an Italian painter of the Renaissance;
or a Greek island, all the buildings are white
except there's too much greenery and mildness.
No way could you make a selection,
choosing this detail and censoring that:
the oil-slick on the water, for example,
or the snubnosed tugboat at the pier
too immediate and unVenetian for comfort.
Dawn is all of a piece, take it or leave it,
and no part of it can be edited out,
especially not the clouds massing over the lake
and darkening the sky minute by minute.
Dear one, it's a seamless whole just as I am
whom I get the feeling you'd like to edit
into a courtesy of green hedges and smooth water,
the oil-slicks and whisky bottles left out
and the tugboat discreetly painted over
or replaced at the mooring by a millionaire's yacht.
Only as a selection can I please you,
as an album – I see it clearly now – of inspiring verse
in covers of expensive tooled leather recalled
from my yearning poetry-hungering adolescence
and now seen only in second-hand bookstores.
And yet, even as an expurgated edition,
the guts and moodiness of me painted out
I'd make a used condom float into your mind
and put a howling into your ears

with grim tales of human villainy you'd rather
you didn't know till you squirmed
and with the prettiest O forming on your mouth
dropped me from your beautiful scalded hands.

OUT OF PURE LUST
for Vivian

The tight sweater she was wearing
showed off her good points at once;
luckily she had an attractive mouth
that lifted my thoughts so that my mind
raced to it from her twin attractions,
settling on neither long enough
to put a glaze on my devouring eyes.

At twenty-one she was explaining for me
why nobody wrote love poems anymore.
"Love's unsatisfied lust, nothing more.
If I want a man I jump into bed with him.
Who needs his heated fantasies, or mine?
I've learned a thing or two about poets:
the only sheets they soil are those they write on.

"If a lover has been fondling my breasts
why should he wish to dream about them
or cudgel his brains to put my nipples into a poem
when he can pop them into his mouth
like ripe berries? I prefer it, mister, that way.
So does he I'm sure, my breasts are so round and firm."
She stopped and I've wondered what old Petrarch would say.

Or lecherous Alighieri who made his Beatrice
immortal by putting his lust into an Inferno.
What if she and Petrarch's Laura had been a good lay
and spoke of their lovers as they might of artichokes,
of ecstasies and fiascos, one-night stands,
finding the comedy of sex too funny for words?
What masterpieces would each have ripped off then?

A body that's dead decays and rots.
Flies gather when it begins to stink
and sages smell no sweeter than sots.
Give heed, peasants, it's later than you think.

For yearning to save a woman's soul
daily he read her some living verse;
but for her the sun and moon were dead
and all that magic was powerless.

A decaying body reeks to heaven
but souls that corrupt smell worse, far worse.
A dead soul takes sweetness from the air,
on life itself lays down its black curse.

He's neither green dragon nor red;
he has lost his connection with the sun.
His lady's soul is dying, is dead,
and there's none can save her now, no one.

NEW SHINING WORLDS
for S. Ross

Solitary
as that lightning-blasted birch
I take comfort from leaves
falling

They tell me nothing
                    endures forever
neither civilizations
nor a woman's malice

Denuding the thicket
leaf by leaf
decay and the punishing minutes
this day
gladden my heart with promise

Only from rot
are new shining worlds begot

The long dark September nights are come,
reminding the vacant poet of losses;
there are no stars in his skull,
only blackness, the fumes of dead loves.

Jerusalem is ruined and pillaged
and her kings and queens are grimacing marionettes.
Where is majesty? Beauty? The courtesies of love?
The stiffening valour in sinew and thigh?

They lie unnoticed on his kitchen floor:
broken pieces of wood, the colours dissolving
into echoes a rising wind amplifies
to a pitch his wearied heart no longer hears.

After each night's solitary meal
he plays blind man's bluff with shadows
that recite lines from his own poems
to mock him as he reaches out hands to touch.

Old poets know that game well.
Designs of soft vulvas cover the walls. Only when
he removes the tight blindfold from his eyes
will a fleshless mouth kiss him with his own passion.

Light on leaves. For me
the most glorious sight earth has to offer.
Greedily I eat, stuffing each bright glitter
into my eyes, always hungering for more.
Who can despair or be unhappy
because he's not seven feet tall
or published in twenty-three languages?

The kitchen's bereft of table and chairs;
white question marks, the cupboard door handles
importune the silence when the radio
stops playing Chopin's sonatas.
The notes lisp and lapse on the stripped walls.

I am alone with my madness and pain.
No voice comes from any part of the house
and all the mirrors in it
are waiting for me to rise from the chair
and release my reflections, one after another,
as I pass from room to empty room.

Nothing is as it was one year ago.
Only the light on twig and leaf is unchanged,
Heraclitus and his flux be damned!
Beauty's radiance is eternal, perfect;
sunlight on leaf will still be here
after I'm gone and taken all my angers with me.
Another bewildered mortal sit
where I am sitting now, perhaps to dream
of the perfect murder, unsolvable as the mystery of creation,
the killer being none other than Oscar Wilde
or the Count of Monte Cristo
come back for his revenges.

My flatted hand descends.
It's too late for him to write his will
or think about estranged wife and friends. Best
just to lie still and keep hoping he'll be able
to hobble to his notary

                  when what's happened's
all over. For now he must
wail till complete awareness returns
and lie, as now, unmoving and quiet
since not yet undazed enough to crawl
to where the smells of mowed grass
are coming from

            or the fine points
of fractured light.

He begins a faint buzz, a feeble stir

                    spins
himself around, once, once more,
like a minuscule coin or turnstile
a hand has twirled into motion

                stops all of a sudden
to get his bearings and rest. Another buzz
this time much louder

           marking out a silence
in which to consider possible meanings.

Was it another insect, larger, more powerful?
The wind that

          when the luck's with him
usually lifts his wings

and escorts him from hedge to hedge?
Perhaps a Fly-God he'd ignorantly overlooked
or hadn't sufficiently flattered or propitiated?

Or, as now seems most likely,
the ledge he was hopping towards when he felt
the sharp thunder at his back
                                    and everything
went suddenly inexplicably black?

He created as warblers sing,
as butterflies mate on white fences.

Delight was his, natural as grass,
as the lovely scents of flowers and logs
after rain. What can vindicate creation
so much as an old delirious man
in love with his life and wife,
the words coming at the right time
to the right beat?

He saw drunks dozing on park benches
or stretched out on sidewalks, asleep.
Happy mortals, he mused, happy, happy mortals,
oblivious of neglect and humiliation,
of all that humans
hold in store for other miserable humans;
to abuse, betrayal, insult
and the raging fires of egotism
in which all must finally char.

His was the joy of self-renewing energy
at war with inertness or that activity
that has possessions for its aim
(another kind of death but one that fools
undertakers who go only by smells).
Now, turned out of that green Eden
he celebrated in poem after poem,
he must listen when inspired lawyers
decode his messages to posterity
or debate its finer points with policemen
and the torpid philistines they protect;

finding himself envying the clochards
snoring on the church steps
and learning a new respect for the hardworking
Niçoise whores he remembers guarding
their corner beats against all newcomers.

SEX APPEAL

When the white-haired poet in despair
turns away from the mindless noise, from
the twitching figures;
        and apocalyptic images
of well-dressed men feasting on babyflesh
        leap into his head
he thinks happily of the neutron bomb,
his face taking on again
        the proud and serene look
that once brought women in their hundreds
        clamouring to his bed

ODD OBSESSION
for Lisa

I've seen your singular smile elsewhere.
On sun-warmed Mediterranean statues
of the late Alexandrian period.

With your fragile, ever-smiling lips you appear
both sensual and ascetic, a coin's toss
sending you either way.

The curves of your mouth bracket your secret.
Which are you? Mary, mother of Jesus,
or that other Mary, the scarlet Magdalene.

Your secret is that you don't know.
So you smile often to conceal your confusion,
giving you that strange look that intrigues us all.

Your lips obsess me like a misremembered word.
I can't remove them from my head, or imagine
any greater triumph than to blot them out forever.

At fourteen I made an older girl
articulate "prunes" over and over again
because her mouth shaped beautifully pronouncing it.

Yours, I finally conclude, is the smile of a woman
who, figure and face making her irresistible,
mocks her lovers' immoderate passion.

But mostly mocks the world and herself,
knowing how brief are the days of beauty;
how cruel and fleeting the loves they inspire.

Banff,
August 15, 1981

For her, sex is something she holds in reserve;
alienated from her real inner self,
it's tended with care like some exotic plant
to allure the stray butterfly to her sill.
She takes Yoga classes and watches what she eats,
is prudent about money and emotions
but unfurls her independence like a flag.
Having been in analysis for insight
(so she informs me) and not therapy
she discusses love as an abstract painting,
a flowing involuted figure by Moore.
She likes catching it out when it makes its spring
and holding its quivering form up to the light,
yet wonders why it blackens and disappears
or grows into some bloated attachment
that mocks her with mouths shaped like grotesque suckers.
An artist in living, she swears by passion
and spontaneity, mistaking fervent
loquacity for something she's too cool,
too cautious to possess, too ungiving
in the modern sense; dismaying the lost men
who circle around her long shapely neck
until they break from the enchantment and run.
It always baffles her she's so much alone
or with old lovers, mostly now with women,
for her mirroring image shows her beautiful
and the great Moore had once praised her talent.
It would be a mercy to make her see
the fault's not entirely hers; it's in the stars,
in the revolving potter's wheel that's sent the sexes
flying off in contrary directions to wander
among sapless words that hang in the air

like stricken November leaves no wind has come
to shake loose. Dry November leaves, my dear,
whose ghostly rattle when a small breeze stirs them
expresses your sad vacancies for the world.

TO MAKE AN END
for Malka Cohen, 1897–1981

The last indignities are over:
the bar between convulsing jaws;
gaunt cheeks, death's familiar foxholes,
and breasts that once gave suck,
now flat and unresponsive as damp rags;
her diminutive teats, raw and wornout,
mocking our vaporous presence on earth
with the mordant emphasis of quotemarks.

If ten devils possessed me
I'd flaunt my scorn for this stale farce
that made Lear and Achilles weep
and pluck those shrivelled paps looking
like forgotten berries on winter's snow;
razor the mortician's balls and grow them
like bleeding rose bulbs in the urine bottle
empty and open to the nurse's hand.

Where's my kinswoman with her blue-black hair,
strong white teeth, peasant health,
her high colour and highboned cheeks?
Is this she, now so shrunk and quiet,
the cannula still in her vein
that supplied her seven rebel parts
till the common axeman
dismissed them all with one soundless blow?

Shall I never touch her warm hand again?
Never again look on her fluttering lids
or praise her rough affection for child and friend?
The white walls are mute. And no clever instrument

waits outside in the blank corridors
to graph incoherency and human rage
or the hopeless, homeless love
of her weeping daughters.

You, Cat, fell for a patrician whore
who scoured the alleyways after dark
looking for an Ethiop's
           hanging ballocks;
fascinatingly evil she was, also witty,
for when told to her face
           she loved cock dearly
she burst out laughing:
"You've said a mouthful."

Still, compared to that broad
your uncle's saddled himself with
           in Verona,
Lesbia's a vestal virgin.
Listen, that jerk your uncle
has got himself a real lulu
           this time:
one eye is without sight
and every morning she startles him awake
with trumpetings
Caesar's legions might envy,
           so dismal is her stomach.
and her teeth – it's the truth, man –
are dissolving in her mouth
           like long icicles,
simply wearing away from her gums
like the shoreline in Calabria.

That's not the end of it, Cat.
Piles ring the darling's asshole
        like a mare's halter
and a flaming herpes
        makes penetration
a risky business.

ZUCCHINI

I'd like my soul to have the same leathery skin
as this zucchini I found in an abandoned basin;
wind and frost have hardened it. I can tell
not even the hottest water will make it edible.

It's spare and curved like an old woman;
long ago it gave up trying to please,
and lies in the moist palm of my hand indifferent
to the amused and pitying look in my eyes.

It accepts its difference without a whimper
or recourse to the big words that pass for wisdom,
especially if they're rhymed or written vertically.
Tough, she's ready for the big blasts. Let them come.

Were I a small child again I'd deck it in hat and shawl
and if its firm spirit didn't terrify me
I'd give it small lustrous eyes
and gouge out a mouth, greying and small.

There, look now: it has dignity with decrepitude.
It's almost as if I held my shrunken mother
in my hands. Nothing could ever content her. Like her
my zucchini spits on the world and is rude.

I'm too fearful to turn my head away.
Only the incantation of some powerful verse
can withdraw me from its demonic sway.
In my entranced ears takes shape a familiar curse.

From poets too I'd like to have direct speech,
no snivelling, each word like a blow.
In rainless deserts the cacti open to the sun
and their perfume is the other language buzzards know.

Boris, you were soft as a boiled potato.
No Hemingway, women had you by your balls
all your life though you had the good sense
to stick with two of them to the very end.
            Apartments of your own divided mind,
you craved to have at once passion and order,
adventure and security; the sure bridge
spanning the terrifying chasm below.
Contrary winds turned you like a weathercock.

Was it weakness made you write the gospel poems,
blubbering at the foot of the Cross
where you'd flung yourself – a baptized unheroic Jew?
Pen for an anti-Semitic vodka-swilling boor
            a shifty unforgivable missive
begging him to let you stay in that foul land
where every lout and time-serving scribbler
might fling his dirt at you,
leer as you wiped the filth from your open face?

Maybe the fault lay in your Jewish genes,
in your terrible need to suffer and to please.
Or was it, after all, only the bored indifference
of transcendent genius that moves always
            on the twin rails of here and beyond, the ideal
and actual, but unerringly to that great good place
where Dr. Zhivago opens its welcoming arms
to seer and sod, revolutionist and pharisee,
and poems stay perfect in the mind of God?

Beautiful, wearing a silver crucifix,
Rosa works in the waterfront bar
as a call girl who does not answer.

All the girls jump from their stools
when the Neapolitans point at them
– but not Rosa.

When the young Mafioso
orders her up to bring his rum and Coke
she offers him the tribute of a slow smile
and takes her time.

Sensing he's different from the others
and knows his worth,
knows he has the sharpest knife
in the city
and two Alsatians that love him.

Naples,
April 15, 1982

What it comes down to, Boris,
is that you're no less a fool
than the rest of us. You love the woman
but you want to be free. You want
to be free but your loins at night
ache and you can't get her face
out of your mind. Your cowardice,
too, is par for the course. Though your life
is hell on earth you won't leave your wife
and go live with the woman you love.
You've got scruples, haven't you? Of course
you have. Build your happiness
on someone else's misery? Not you, Boris.
That would betray the favourite snapshot
you have of yourself, the one you cling to
most ferociously when you're being pulled
from all sides. So you meet clandestinely
in her room to snatch an embrace before
your lover throws another of her tantrums
or the squabbling begins. Since you own
the merciless self-awareness of the poet,
no one knows better than yourself how silly
are the excuses you make while exhibiting
in almost equal proportion tenderness, candour,
and heartlessness, knowing in the end
your innocent charm will get you off the hook
and earn for you her forgiving smile. Why?
Because the lady is young and nuts
about you, even when you flap about
like loose awning in the storm of words
you let fall on her dear head so you won't hear
your own self-contempt gnawing at your vitals;

even when you're a pitiful caricature
of the ideal poet whose image you carry
in your head and betray with each word or deed
and even, as now, with the very silence
in which your next poem is taking form.

To go with genius
        the whole distance
is to walk straight into Thanatos
with a greeting smile
        to match his own.

Hard to come that near to death;
harder still
        not to frown.

Death cut him down like a tall pine
after letting him hack his lungs out
with TB. I well remember his blue eyes,
his aquiline nose; Roman I'd have said
had I been Miss Thorpe's pupil in Grade Nine
but I was barely eleven when he died
and Caesar not even a name. Pompey neither.
I, at least, had the warrant of age
but my other brothers seemed runts when they
walked beside him so very tall he was
– tall and straight as a woodland pine
but each day growing more peremptory,
more fractious and unlovable as he wasted
under the white blankets my mother bleached
and ironed for him day after day.
                                        And so,
after they'd washed his body and robed him
in his cerements he was too long for the coffin
and I watched, horrified, from my safe hole
two voiceless men lean on his knob to push
it down, making the stiffened feet jump up
as though he were a runner preparing
for an Olympic track or a harlequin,
full of inventive tricks, about to appear
for the crowd's applause. Now another pair,
blackbearded and waiting in silence
at the casket's other end, shoved
his feet in (I still hear their
scraping sound against the board)
and I saw his head rise up suddenly
like that of a drowning man surfacing to take
one final look before going down forever.

Again

they pressed down on his skull, this time hard,
and the bare rodlike feet flew out
above the planed edge of the bone box ready,
it seemed, to walk on air or to start
running, so forceful had been their thrust
into the fetid, overheated room. It surprised me
to see them halted in mid-air, stiff and white
as if they'd already turned to chalk. It didn't
look right somehow and though damp all over,
a fine chill went down my back and I began
to retch loudly, exposing me all at once
to eyes that flew at me like released wasps.

Now

that I'm far away from that strange hour
I'm more prudent or luckier as to where
I find my metaphors for life and death,
those fragments of lived experience
a man converts into consolatory hints
or the needed culm for self-propulsion
towards the paling stars, or for self-excuse:
yet can't quite empty my imagination
of the ludicrous seesaw that finished only
when they crooked my brother's unoiled knees,
afterwards banging the coffinlid tight
while I prayed for the wordless attendants
to begin their morning devotions,
turning whiter than his cooled corse
before tightlipped with fear I bolted
for the familiar kitchen smells
and the rude affection in my mother's hands.

Your warty lads are too shy to tell you
they burn to cover your body full length.

But I, a white-haired lecher and famous,
boldly apprise the world I do.

Dear maid, which will pleasure you most:
a young man's shyness or an old man's lust?

KALI IN THE SUBURBS

On the cluttered kitchen table
she has left for his morning meal
the fragrance he loves

She has also left
three half-slices of dark toast,
some cheese with knife bladed like a dagger,
handle black and made from rubber;
the ebony contours of coffee making

Piggy that didn't go to market,
the honey's plastic container
sits like a porcine Buddha
poised between smugness and serenity;
the light-brown viscous honey
fills shaped mouth and snout

The confined sweetness the light outlines
barely touches the earlobes;
bland are the eyes, unclouded,
that fix on him their forceless stare

GREEK FLY

Wings filled with divine inner chaos

Bringing bouzouki music to chairs, walls, tables
and the long thin ouzo glasses on the table
or taking its inspired frenzies up to the ceiling,
spotted picture frames and oleographs
or to the taciturn wife and husband whose day
begins with their disappointment in each other

Rubbing the golden moments between its legs
the rapturous fly comes to rest on a nail
making it buzz with the unceasing malice
of an old woman's tongue: the kitchen
is loud with its dry bright-hued gossip and abuse;
then landing on my shoulder the fly announces
to saucepans, forks, still uneaten eggs
and to all the crumbs the splendid news
that like my vaccinated arm my poems
are good for all borders

Shifting to another fleshly promontory
it stands on one leg like a proud Talmudic scholar
and recites the entire *Odyssey*
and is about to begin the *Iliad*
when catching sight of itself in the mirror
it leaps into the air like Nureyev
and gives a breath-taking performance
of a fly chasing itself until it's caught

The fly brings ripe hayfields into the room
the smell of cows and summer barnyards
the innocence of children clapping their hands in play

Mao and the Chinese revolution that sent it here
and all the poems ever written about mortality
and Emily dying to its ever fainter buzz;
head between its legs it thinks hard about life's brevity
then like a mad Euripidean Greek it drops
a billion eggs to fertilize its unkillable tragic splendour

It takes chances, this fly, like a poet;
it threads the air under the wife's frown
and recklessly settles on her puckered forehead
as if it were the face of Papadopoulos lying in his coffin
then shamelessly cleans its legs before her eyes
when her loathing for her husband in her open palm
descends on it with all the unerring ferocity
of repressed lasciviousness and thirteen years
of successful marriage

There it lies on the floor
waiting for the funeral orations to begin

Molibos, Lesbos,
August 6, 1973

270

Madman, born to strife as sparks fly upward.
A martyr to rapture and swift revulsion,
woman was the weight you bore, her soft limbs
around your neck, her hands gripping your hair.

Your discarded wives? Ecstasies you suffered
till suffering became your ecstasy,
the healthful dram of poison in your dramas.
You played with marriages as a child with blocks.

Giddyap! Giddyap up to the heights. Whipping you
with epiphanies welts alone can yield,
Hecate lashed you on to greatness.
Now men live more sanely for your madness.

Morality's a cloak for neurosis, you raged;
the sinner's delighting reek of guilt
consoles mankind for its fall from grace.
Men must clean their hands in their neighbour's blood.

For life's a cess in woman's lovely crotch
where's sown Christ's crown of spikes and thorns.
Every poet must find his Magdalene
who when he's dead will cry his resurrection.

August Strindberg. Brutal wars with women
exhausted him and he forgot his atheism
and despair, forgot the sentimental red-eyed demons
that cast their nets for the human soul. Guilts
will rot a man worse than syphilis.
                                    At the end,
closing his eyes he mumbled pieties
heard at his mother's knee,
clutching a mournful tinplate Jesus to his breast.
AVE CRUX SPES UNICA

After the cocktails and compliments
men turn wolves, women bare their serpent fangs.
Kazantzakis, too, crowed like chanticleer,
crowed once and fell silent,
numbed by the stellar chill, the vacuity
human swarms make
beneath immense star clusters moving in empty space.
                                    At life's close,
comfortless as a newborn babe he too sank back
into the primal womb. Come, my enamoured friends,
let us pluck splinters
from the stolid cross sprouting from his pierced heart.

San José,
March 3, 1984

ELEGY FOR MARILYN MONROE

Last summer, it was "Papa" Hemingway
This summer it's Marilyn Monroe
Next summer, who? – Who will it be?
But Orville Faubus gets re-elected
Two hundred million X-Laxed Americans
          go on defecating as before
and Congress acts as if nothing had happened.

How come I asked of Lyndon Johnson
          there's no Committee
to investigate
the high rate of suicide
among those with a tragic overplus
of sensitivity and consciousness;
and received a postcard
          showing a Texan oil field.

Gentlemen, take it for what it's worth
but I suspect something more terrible
          than radioactive fallout
or the unmentionable gases of Belsen
has penetrated our human atmosphere.
The PTA's haven't heard of it yet
or the Board of Directors of Bell Tel
or President Kennedy;
moreover if I manoeuvred to let them know
          what it is
there'd be a Congressional committee
to investigate me!
They'd get cracking at once. O yes.

You ask, what is it
that goes straight for its victims like radar?
I name it the Zed-factor,
lethal only to the passionate, the imaginative,
          and to whatever is rare and delightful
in this brute universe.

Invisible as halitosis or body odour
it makes no warning of its presence;
therefore no T.V. outfit
will sing commercials to it
with chuckling hooligans
          poking fingers through plugged drains,
and anyhow since only an infinitesimal part
of the nation
is susceptible to attack
why bother? See, why bother?

Good-bye Marilyn
It's raining in Magog
          a town you probably never heard of
where I sit in a tavern writing this;
nor did you ever hear of me
though I once composed a whole poem to you
and called you "Earth Goddess."
The janitors to whom you said hello,
the cabbies who spotted you by your stride
          and magnificent blonde hair
and whistled and honked their horns
to let you know their good luck,
the men all around the world
who touched your limbs in irreverent sleep
will miss your wiggle and crazy laugh,
but no one more than I
dazed this afternoon by grief and drink;

for I loved you from the first
who know what they do not know,
seeing in your death a tragic portent
for all of us who crawl and die
under the wheeling, disappearing stars;
and who must now live with the self-complacent,
      the enduring dull,
without your sustaining radiance,
your rarity.

From here on in
they have it, the pygmies have it,
it's all theirs!

Good-bye Marilyn
Sleep, sleep peacefully tonight,
One poet at least will remember
      your brightness,
the unique fever in your form and face
(O insuperable filament, now black, now ash!)
and love you always.

Your first mural brought religion
back into the church. The bishop ground
his expensive teeth and groaned aloud
seeing how you praised the living God
but the rude villagers who came to pray stayed.
Yours was the prophet's art they saw
that exalting the humble humbled the proud.

Now instead of Nazi bombs and suffering saint
it's unquiet landscapes your skilled hand paints,
bringing to the viewer no relief, no rest:
nature for you is the primal terrorist
more fearsome than the swaggering fascist
who for all his power and strut must one day die
and beneath her indifferent sward lie.

I like the laughter of your wild white roses,
your hollyhock and thistle and chicory.
I hear it above the gloom and doom of your dark lawns
where two bushes plot an assassination,
three are a conspiracy to bring down the government.
Each man makes his own arrangements with death. Dear friend,
one day you will bury him in one of your landscapes.

Why are the birds flying overhead?
Do they make out the waves to be rotting heads?
Do they smell black carrion drifting on the sea?
The midday sun is in the sky,
throwing down his small silver horseshoes
that land near the bobbing heads and floating corpses.
The dog that was friendly yesterday
frantically scoops the sand with his forepaws
as if he were thirstily digging for water
and covers my books and papers with it. He never stops.
I notice a mysterious swarm of flies
where the children are building castles and moats.
A small boat chugs past. A water-skier
alights suddenly as if from nowhere
like an angel come to warn us. Of what?
I fear the worst, brothers and friends.
The calm sea, the blue sky, the laughing children
are deceptions. I tell you I smell burning wood.
I see and hear sizzling flesh, the hissing oils and fats
start fires in the streets.
Tall buildings sway and totter like old men
before they crumble into a waterfall of bricks.
The cries and moans never cease.
The cities of the plain are burning.
London. Berlin. Vienna. Warsaw. Moscow.
Night after night, they blaze like enormous faggots
against the lowering sky.
A hideous smell of gas covers Europe from end to end.
When the cities have burned themselves out
the heavens will open up

and black torrential rains will descend for forty days
and forty nights.
Everything alive is submerged and drowned.
I see no tossing ark.

BOSCHKA LAYTON: 1921–1984

Because each act of creation is a miracle
that happens again and again
until it becomes familiar as an autumn leaf
or a ripening apple tree in full sail

I shall remember you not as charred bone and ash
to be given to earth's mad alchemy
but as the full-bosomed woman whose lips
mouthed my awed whisper: "We shall make handsome children"

Your heart's vital joy apparent in the eyes of friends,
in children's smiles and the smiles of old women,
it is presumptuous to speak now of your crazy defiance
idle to praise the harsh devotions of your life

Ordinary miracles to pry open the eyes of the blind
happen every day. Yet my deep faith holds:
sun, wind, rain, and the dark nights will change
my Boschka's cinders to deathless apples and poems

Santa Rosa,
February 17, 1984

The sleepwalkers are advancing on Armageddon
where the lines form for the final conflict;
they all smile beatifically over
their shopping bags, their hands covered
by diamonds and fresh blood.
A few dash into the fray still wet
from their pools and surfing. Finally,
after the last shriek has died away
the smoke clears over another Stone Age,   .
over cave dwellers and humans with painted skins:
cannibals devour each other's kidneys and brains.

Another Megiddo rises, another Troy. Again
satyrs link tails and dance in the moonlight,
another Abram hears injunctions the wind utters
or a tapestry fluttering against a wall
and forthwith quits the valley of his forefathers
to begin the tragic husking of mankind,
the reformation of a brute universe
in all its parts by sentience and love;
always his heirs will climb towards the same ruin
until this creation becomes one vast inertness
with not a single mind to know its doom.

Until yesterday I knew nothing about elephants
        except their slowness to mate;
this morning, in a Nepalese village, while I sat out
        the rain in a wayside shrine,
a riderless elephant slowly made his way
        towards one of the ancient trees
lining the street and there began to scrape
        his immense slate-coloured flank
against the rough, knobby bark of a similar greyness
        and toughness; forward and back,
forward and back, as if bent on sawing down the tree
        with one side of his belly;
keeping somehow as much of a clown's sad,
        self-conscious dignity
as humiliating circumstance might allow,
        yet his bull posture
plainly spelling it out: blows, ridicule, men's
                                   displeasure
        are wind beneath his ears;
nothing will drive him from this ecstasy rotundity
        and gratuitous weight
make proportionate to his itch, this rapturous blare
        under his vast hide unwrinkling
like a flower.

Look at that wise, old sybarite!
        The creaking tree says it
for him, and the leaves of the tree
        like multiple green tongues:
"A-ah" "A-ah" "A-ah" "A-ah" until the birds
        nesting or resting among them

take it up and translate it into song;
        unhurriedly, methodically
like an old woman washing herself in the morning
        he does the other side of his belly
which now hangs like a big, grey globe of the world;
        then comes the turn
of his nolessitchy behind though his absurd tail
        fouls his sexy stripper's act;
and lastly that of his hind legs, each time making
                              me think
        he has three of them.
He moves his head to let me take in the roguish humour
        in his eyes, the ironic
and quietly exultant smile of someone who has learned
        the necessary art
of converting irritation into pleasure
        and giving a final flick of his tail,
a disdainful yet gentle "that's it" or "that's all
                        for now"
        lumbers off as mysteriously
as he came, leaving me with this poem.

FUNERARIA "OLEA"

In bold black letters
SERVICIO DIA Y NOCHE
Obviously this is not a dead business.

It is a thriving business.
Go in,
See for yourself the white coffins
Lying in wait for the townspeople.

The tiniest caskets
Are the most numerous;
The women in these parts
Are always pregnant with them.

Zihuatanejo, Mexico

Moving slow and gorgeous
as in the feathered radiance
of a dream
and without defence
as Beauty and Delight
always have been,
he's the poet among birds

Only in a cage
where he can strut and astound
is he secure
from claws and fangs
indifferent
to the elegant loveliness
of his elongated vulnerable tail

Pride-besotted creature
to have so many eyes
and to be so blind

MUSIC HATH SUCH CHARMS
for Marc Bernstein

Handel composed the MESSIAH
and loved the whores.
Bach was sent to jail for bribery.
Jean Baptiste Lully, thief and swindler,
scored masses and Te Deums:
also with the Princesses of the court.
Corelli was a glutton;
Liszt, a vain seducer.
Carlo Gesualdo who strangled his son
who poisoned his father
and killed his wife
wrote exquisite madrigals
all his life.

He showed me his painting of the Po,
canvas after canvas after canvas
until I thought he was out
to drown me in his studio.
Then he switched to nudes. Again it was
canvas after canvas but now they were
all of the same young woman whose hair
he coloured differently, each time
doing some altering thing
to her neck or mouth. He'd painted her
earthy and withdrawn, sensual,
a far-away look in her grey eyes.
Yet what I remember are not the soft
pastel shades, the disciplined tints
in river and woman, or how I kept thinking
the river could be the woman's unshed tears.
No, what stays in my mind is the silence
that filled the cluttered room
after he had finished speaking
and the terrible sadness for which
there are no words, no colours anywhere.

FELLINI

Like the *guardiacessi* who unlocks her toilet
and is deformed but has a winning face
you show me the grossness in earth, in women,
but also the shy soft-hued floweret
among thistles, the ugly rapacious thistles.

Your legends, Federico, I've made my own;
amidst them often lost, often found my way.
Basta! You use my skull to hive your images.
Casanova's mother piggybacks to this day;
your spiritless bird will endure longer than stone.

Master illusionist you are, every sunrise,
the exploring poet in your own *Satyricon*
seeking the light of remoter shores
to tell their bronzed surfers the Gods urge on
only the cripples that stumble to Paradise.

Your felicity, when it comes, is more brief
than the bubbles you loose over these ancient stairs;
perilous is the fate you were meant to bear:
by art alone to modulate human grief
into a cry so sad, so strange, men call it rapture.

Piazza di Spagna,
September 17, 1984

FINAL RECKONING: AFTER THEOGNIS

Me? I feel safest in cemeteries.
Horizontal humans lie peacefully;
no anger or mischief in them, no hate
and deceit. Even if darkness comes
when I find myself standing near a slab
time and fierce squalls have tilted towards me
so that I think of the moles underfoot
tearing the flesh clean off the skeletons
I have no fear or sadness. Why should I?
The dead are surely more fortunate
to be done at last with life's ills and chills,
with the lies needed for mere survival
and the mean compromises each must make
before he can call some small space his own.
Bah! the comedy's not worth a frog's fart;
only priests and rabbis think otherwise,
metaphysicians and crazed Bolsheviks.
For myself, I love the tranquil boneyards
both for the evergreen moral they teach
and for the asylum they give against
the violent longings that agitate
the caged animals of Chicago
and Madrid, of Moscow, Belfast and London.
Tombs, I say, are reassuring when men
are swine, smiling wolves with capped teeth,
the cities reeking of scribbling whores
and those who need no bribes to pimp for them.
To these, O Zeus, send plagues! Destroy them all!
Don't leave behind a single specimen

and rid earth of locusts, snakes, and weevils;
let the new seedlings come up tall and green.
Preserve all poets mad and marvellous,
guard them from the fury of envious dust.

It's when he's drunk
that he knows he should never be married
or have children;
what has he to do
with the conversation of wives
or the chatter and nosepickings of children?

He should be a cloud, a forest fragrance,
a startled fawn, at one
with the elemental force
that makes a plantain leaf
fall to the ground
or a peacock spread its tail to the sun

Where is he? Tall and muscular,
he went into the ring
to beat the brains out of his opponent;
afterwards when he leaned over me
like the tower of Pisa
his grey eyes laughed.

Why after half a century
won't his image leave me? Does
repressed envy lie dormant like a seed
to ripen again and again
like immortelles?

Is he still living?
Did he have a good life? Father sturdy children?
Make some woman happy
despite the odds against that happening?
Or did he end up
a used-up executive in Niagara-on-the-Lake,
obese and disgruntled?

Perhaps he's at the golf links
where I'll find him swinging a club.
If I recognize him
what shall I say?

Why does his imagined face
so move me
after all these years?

Niagara-on-the-Lake,
September 15, 1982

OLD MEN

At 4 A.M.
the mind washes its dirty linen.
Hopeless. It will never get it clean.
Till the late hour counsels resignation.

Unless one's gifted
with indignation and laughter
life's one long accumulation
of griefs and guilts,
stains put there by body and spirit.

Have you known old men
muttering to themselves, hawking and spitting?
That's the soul's sour phlegm they're tasting,
sometimes wiping it on their sleeve
sometimes giving it to the wind.

Old men,
they alone have my charity
mumbling hapless and broken
in the toils of their memories.

THE LESSON

This is a finger
This is an eye

Even a small cut causes pain, afterwards soreness;
the terror comes when a bone-shattering bullet
enters the neck, the groin
or the blood rushes after the retreating knife

The thought of death,
of being suddenly reduced to nothing,
makes the lips go white

You must say to yourself
this is not film, this is real
and it's happening to a man
who was once an infant and cried in the dark

Those are real intestines
spilling out into his hand;
the pain and terror are real

Let's begin again
This is a finger
This is an eye

BOTTLES
for Giorgio Morandi

In Bologna
I learned of an artist
who'd painted only bottles.
The *ristorantes* must have been
crowded and noisy
as they are now
and the expensive shops
filled with priceless things
only money can buy
but he painted only bottles.
He must have seen
the ancient churches and squares,
the famous university and monuments;
he must have eaten
prosciutto, salamis, tortellini
and drunk the sparkling wines
of Bologna:
but he painted only bottles.
Mussolini came and went,
likewise the war,
Hiroshima, the Holocaust,
Stalin, the smooth displacement of culture
by pornography:
he painted only bottles
and one famous self-portrait.
There must be a deep meaning
in this somewhere
but what it is
I cannot tell

but must wait for instruction
from a wise old whore,
a philosopher
or death at my bolted door.

ARABS

The world's last poets
in love with hyperbole and disaster:
        eloquent romantics
Inshallah, malesh, bukra
In the beginning was the word
        which, prepotent,
exorcises tanks and planes,
annihilates machines and skilled mechanics.

Ah, my word-intoxicated brothers,
        for your faith
going down to defeat, to misery and misfortune
with the sad fatalism
        of a Verlaine,
how can I not love you:
you who cling so beautifully
        to a tradition
that refuses to turn lathes for you
or operate motors and drills;
you who pave the floors
        of your dark hovels
with a mosaic of dreams
proud lovers, poets, scholars, and astronomers
tread upon in all their remembered brightness.

The 20th century
ticks in all the ominous corners
        of your unswept courtyards:
"you are not contemporary, go away"
and in your defeat
        I see my own
as destiny picks you up

still muttering to the indifferent air
"*Inshallah, malesh, bukra*"
      and like one of Omar's chessmen
puts you one by one silently away.

Hellenes
Alcaeus and Sappho might have known
to love or spurn
once lived here;
ate olives and quince, drank wine,
fought and died

And brave conquerors came
and were conquered,
killed and bled
on the same stones
the Aegean still washes, wave upon wave:
Saracen, Genoese, Venetian, Turk

Before dusk has fallen on them
I have stared,
stared and wondered: whose blood
makes so red
the damask roses
burning in my courtyard?

Molibos, Lesbos,
July 23, 1977

I wake from a troubled doze and rub my eyes.
The Jew is still whispering his tribal secrets
to the wall, bending his spare frame this way
and that, almost licking the Hebrew words off their page.

The same human carnage flows through his veins as mine,
yet I turn from him in sadness and dismay. He's one
of God's white mice in whose damaged bodies
vaccines are made for the select few, immunizing

Them against a world Divine Justice
made purposely malign. Though his skin's pallor
and burning speechless gaze mark out the fanatic,
the lobby's glare despoils him of mystery and love.

The lighted lobby turns everything commonplace,
diminishes the most barbarous event into a happening
in search of a camera while saints and holy men
beseech the deaf walls for favours and I

God's recording angel loosed in a roaring desert
gape at the blind lens like a once famous Alpinist
whose name we recall only after a long wooden pause,
a flurry of precipitous promptings.

"*Ghetto of the elect. A wall, a ditch.*
Expect no mercy. In this most Christian
of worlds, the poet is a Jew."
                              — Marina Tsvetayeva

Her motions are off-key;
the unused limbs quiver.
It's apparent she does not know
the steps to the Greek dance.
But her wild eyes close in a trance
and every black inch
of her festive body
is alive with *kefi*.

When she seizes the hem
of her dress, showing pocked thighs,
the island gods are happy.
So is every mortal
in the *kafénion*,
for her tremulous flesh is on fire,
and the flame licks her
till she melts like wax.

Her clumsy, joyous dancing
burns away chains and gyves,
makes of form itself a ruinous blaze.
The fire, only the fire matters,
the impulse in awakening seed.
When she leaves, taking her dark skin,
the lit place loses radiance
and we become patient mortals again.

Tinos,
May 15, 1985

ON THE DEATH OF POPE PAUL VI

An animal dies
and rots back into the earth

Vanquished crustaceans
are washed up by the tide

A swordfish is hooked
and turned to faeces and gas

But a pope greets Monsignor Death
with a mitre on his head

Red slippers on his feet

And formaldehyde in his veins

LA CONDITION HUMAINE

And yet I wonder
which gave Camus
the greater angst:

Life's pointless suffering
and the viciousness
of the human race

Or that a protruding ear
spoiled his good looks?

Doktor Marx
    old swarthy rabbin face
        ferule behind your back
           to crack knuckles with
Is this what you wanted?
    dilapidated run-down lives
        nosing out valuta and your famous
           Manifesto under a grubby deck of cards
Because the perfect revolution
    (yours) has been made
        and now there's nothing else
           to do with one's life?

Listen, you Prussian asshole
    the funky aristos
        hated equality
           more than the pox
But everything beautiful
    in this city
        was their idea
Though castles churches palaces gracious parks
    do look like amnesiacs
        trying to recall something
           in the pallid sunshine
And elegance is a feeble old woman
    selling flowers
        in the marketplace,
A bygone irretrievable beauty
    IBUSZ and the proles exploit
        while posing as experts
           on the bowel movements of history

Which is alright with me, Herr Marx,
    as long as you and they
        let me know in good time
            which way the wind's blowing
For my impartiality
    between whites and reds
        is you may believe me
            nothing less than godlike

A poet's colours
    are green and black
        the colours of life and death
And his Internationale begins:
    let's all fart in the ears
        of commissars and priests
And I'm here
    in this faded city only
        because I hope to find
            behind all these scurrying bones
                one unfearing authentic man

IBUSZ is the Hungarian Travel Agency

With the money I spend on you
I could buy ice cream for Korean kings.
I could adopt a beggar
     and clothe him in scarlet and gold.
I could leave a legacy of dolls and roses
     to my grandchildren.
Why must you order expensive Turkish cigarettes?
And why do you drink only the most costly champagne?
The Leninists are marching on us.
Their eyes are inflamed with social justice.
Their mouths are contorted with the brotherhood of man.
Their fists are heavy with universal love.
They have not read a line of Mayakovsky's poems
     for twelve whole months.
The deprivation has made them desperate.
With staring eyeballs they hold off
     waiting for the ash from your cigarette to fall.
That is the signal.
When the ash crumbles, the man with the tallest forehead
     will smash a cracked hourglass, the sound
          amplified into a thousand manifestos.
Can you not see them? Can you not hear them?
Already they are closing in on us.
Your fragrant body means nothing to them.
Under your very eyes, velvet and remarkable,
     they intone that Beauty is not absolute.
They shout for an unobstructed view of your shoulders,
     your proud and beautiful head gone.
They will break your arms and slender legs
     into firewood.
The golden delicate hairs I have kissed
     into fire a thousand times

will blaze more brightly;
But who will bend down to gather the flames
        into their mouth?
Who will follow their white light into eternity?

Because I love you better
        than artichokes and candles in the dark,
I shall speak to them.
Perhaps they will overlook your grace for my sake,
        ignore the offending perfection of your lips.
Perhaps, after all, you and I will start
        a mass conversion into elegance.
I will tell them my father made cheese
        and was humble and poor all his life,
And that his father before him turned ill
        at the mere sight of money;
And that a certain ancestor of mine
        never saw money at all,
                having been born blind.
On my mother's side, they were all failures.
Calliopes will sound for my undistinguished lineage
And the aroused Leninists will at once guess
        I am a fool in love, a simpleton,
                an ensnared and deranged proletarian
With no prospects but the wind which exposes
        my terrible hungers to them,
My counter-revolutionary appetite to be lost
        from all useful labour
                in your arms hair thighs navel;
And parting the clouds, one solitary star
        to show them where I am slain
Counting the gold coins
        for your Turkish cigarettes and costly champagne.

As the angry hawk flies towards the sun,
Taking some small creature into the skies,
So shall your fame be taloned fast to mine
And like the clawed rodent rise as I rise.

ATTENDING SUZANNE'S FUNERAL

I just can't take it in
that what I'm looking at
        is your cadaver,
recalling your abundant health
and glistening eyes avid for more life,
the strong sensitive fingers
        that probed for tubers
in the frozen Siberian ground.

This late afternoon
it's cold comfort
        to tell myself
you always enjoyed a good laugh
and now may be sleeping off
the genial cups of wine
you shared last night with a friend
solitary as yourself
in London Ont.,
        pulling a long face
only to give Death back
some of his own gloom.

With so much dignity in your mien
and a touch of your mother's primness,
it's plain you want to go on
treating that boor
as though he were
one more interrogator,
one more Soviet flunky
        eliciting as always
your absolute silence
your tightlipped disdain

for his peasant gaucheness
as you snap, my dauntless Suzanne,
this last chain of illusion
　　　　　and break away
finally and forever free.

Almost ten years have gone by since I first came to this village.

The same smells from the fields, the same breezes from the sea.

The same stars that have shot up and down that blue patch
of sky above me.

The cypresses rising up in the dark like tall solitary madmen
muttering to themselves about the night's intolerable sultriness.

The post office to my left, the garbage-collector's house to my
right.

My feet make the same eerie crunch-sounds, I breathe a little
heavier.

Under the white stars I carry in my headpiece the same unshakable
faith in the holiness of reason, beauty and love.

And in the same fragile headpiece the memory of affections,
enmities, ambitions, the cruel words heard and said, the shameful
deeds, and the glory of breasting the evil hours like a ship's prow.

My disenchantment with the human race that has hardened like
cement or settled like a freshly dug grave over which hovers a
single butterfly.

Revolutions, wars, assassinations, and the deaths of great and
famous men – all the familiar troubles. And explorations into
space to find God wandering among the galaxies and to bring
him back to his creatures dying of loneliness and anomie.

Behind me, the same frenzied tourists in the *kafénions* wearing different clothes and faces, the same rueful Greek merchants rubbing their smiles together to strike fire from them, *kefi*.

Ahead of me, the same winding road on which you halt for a moment to gaze thoughtfully at the moon-polished sea and the small white-walled cemetery that in the distance looks like a gleaming skull someone has playfully rolled down into the valley.

Asthmatic and always stuffing your face;
Your lymph glands brimming with chemicals to control
Unavailingly your adiposity and sinister wheezings;
The sudden breathlessness that threatened each time
To unhook your fat body from your soul. . . .

You've taken the whole works into the grave
With you. After all the noisy convulsive shakes
Like those of a resistless locomotive rumbling
Out of the station – silence. Uncanny silence.
Not a single wheeze can ever startle you awake.

Death, the fathead, struck you when you were alone;
Stabbed that great heart of yours, sparing
The mediocrities and prudent losers you scorned.
So many lumps to choose from, their numbers increasing,
And that dull jerk must come and strike you down.

My dear incomparable Lilli, I find it strange to think
I shall never again hear your indecorous wit
Or see your wide luminous eyes glitter with humour
And affection. Unencumbered, now lighter than air
My fat companionable pole-vaulter, you leave the ground and soar.

BIRTHDAY POEM FOR JOHN NEWLOVE

All poets are magicians or murderers;
the indeterminate end up editing magazines
or working at Harbourfront.
Here prayers and connections are useless.

I can only speak for myself.
Still, when I read your verse
I feel you've looked on the Medusa face of love
and seen, yes, the glory and horror
in that gorgon's bloodshot eyes;
better than most
you know the awful price
a masterpiece exacts,
you having paid it oftener
than Trudeau has sniffed his red *boutonnière*.

I watched you lug around for years
your disappointment in God and yourself,
your pity for the lonely old men
fumbling towards their death
in libraries and public toilets.
Your opulent despair
at what we yahoos do to ourselves
– more often than not I share it.

But you don't leave me there forever;
there's also your enormous zest
for the different tonalities of noise
(grey music you call some of it)
"Were the bunks neat in Auschwitz?" you ask.

I can also imagine you laughing
at the fastidious copulation of spiders.

Whom the gods do not intend to destroy
they first make mad with poetry.

SANDCRAB

On the wide vacant beach
I've blocked the entry
to his house;
he freezes with dismay
and I sense his panic
is no less
than that of the poet
who watches his abused talent
draining away
and with it his one excuse
to keep back self-contempt
and mindless death.

ETRUSCAN TOMBS

for Dante Gardini

Being so close to death
so many times
why should you be moved, as I am,
by these offenceless ruins?

I ask pardon for my abstracted gaze,
my impatience with your slow speech,
your gentle all-forgiving smile.
I did not spend my best years
in a concentration camp;
no vile humanoid ever
menaced me with gun and whip
or made me slaver for crusts
urine-soiled and stale;
no officered brute made me kneel in shit.

Here beside you in this remote scene
I feel death's cold finger on my skin,
making it twitch like a fly-stung mare's.
Yet these blank eyes sculpted
from grove and hill and rock
before which the centuries have passed unseen
comfort me; inuring me, I say,
to the sorrows our humanity
compels us to inflict on each other.
They teach me to live the free hours with gusto.

Nothing endures forever.
Your pain, my pleasure,
the seconds bear away;

our flesh, Dante, one day
will be such golden dust
as a storyless wind stirs
in an empty vault.

Norchia,
September 18, 1984

King David, flushed with wine,
  is dancing before the Ark;
the virgins are whispering to each other
and the elders are pursing their lips
  but the king knows the Lord delights
in the sight of a valorous man
dancing in the pride of life.

For the Lord of Israel sometimes
  also reels on drunken feet: see,
in the wayward flight of eagles and moths,
in thunderstorms and when lightning
  rives the cedars of Lebanon,
O the Lord wheels in blazing footgear
above the hills of Jerusalem.

King David is circling the Ark
  on reeling feet, and he sings:
"Ho, Israelites, hear me! Hear me, everyone!
God himself staggers on drunken feet
  and each night wearing
for raiment the flame of our campfires
He dances in our valleys North and South!"

Black-bearded stalwarts leap up to follow him
  as he stumbles around the Ark;
no one listens, none in the throng is fired
with his wild peculiar joy. So bowing low
  he kisses the Ark thrice
and with a last joyous cry reels singing to his tent
to compose a boisterous hymn in praise of the Lord.

IRVING LAYTON ON POETRY

What insight does the modern poet give us into the absolute evil of our times? Where is the poet who can make clear for us Belsen? Vorkuta? Hiroshima? The utter wickedness of Nazism and National-Communism? There is no poet in the English-speaking world who gives me the feeling that into his lines have entered the misery and crucifixion of our age. His psychology, pre-Freudian; his political thought, pre-totalitarian; his metaphysics, non-existent, his well-meant blabbings originate in a bourgeois-Christian humanism totally unable to account for the vilenesses enacted by men and women of this century. Does the aestheticism of Pound explain them? The sweat-less paganism of Wallace Stevens? Innocency, naïveté, the decencies and dullnesses of the clergyman. Nowhere is the image of man portrayed that might have stiffened us for the cruelty, perversion, systematic lying, and monstrous hypocrisy of the totalitarian regimes of Hitler's Germany and Stalin's Russia, or the no less damnable perversions and hypocrisies of the European bourgeois and imperialists. When I say nowhere, I mean nowhere in poetry. Turn to the novel or the play, and the frightful hideousness of contemporary man is their constant theme and preoccupation. Man, without a soul; man, robotized; man, tortured, humiliated, and crucified; man, driven into slave camps and death factories by devils and perverts; man, the dirtiest predator of all. The novelists: Kafka, Dostoievsky, Lawrence, Faulkner; the playwrights: Beckett, Genet, Ionesco – almost every page of theirs is a condemnation and a warning. The poets? Pound's mid-Western blat about Social Credit? Eliot's weary Anglicanism? Yeats's fairy-tale Byzantium? In these vicious, revolutionary times? Don't make me laugh. Frost's jaunty pastoralism? Auden's sensationalistic mishmash of psychoanalysis, Marxism, and Christianity? What a sour, boring joke!

With only a few exceptions – Lawrence, Rimbaud – the modern poet has been an empty windbag and a chatterer. No wonder anguished people turn from him in amusement, boredom, or pity. He has nothing to say worth listening to. One asks for bread and is given a plethora of sounds. The major poets are children lost in a painted forest, making as much noise as they can to attract attention; the lesser ones absent-mindedly continue bringing their posies into the swept courtyards of Auschwitz and Belsen; all of them intent on proving to the world how sensitive they are, how perceptive, how erudite and archetype-crammed. The truth is this: instead of remembering they are prophets and the descendants of prophets, the poets have swapped roles with entertainers and culture-peddlers.

("Foreword," *Balls for a One-Armed Juggler*, 1963)

* * *

I now see there is no way for the poet to avoid misunderstanding, even abuse, when he follows his prophetic vocation to lead his fellowmen towards sanity and light. If he offers his hand in friendship and love, he must expect someone will try to chop it off at the shoulder. Sentimentality to pretend such things do not happen. A poet is someone who has a strong sense of self and feels his life to be meaningful. By insisting on that self and refusing to become the socialized article that bureaucrats, priests, rabbis, and so-called educators approve of, the poet offends the brainwashed millions who are the majority in any country. His words, his free manner of living, are a constant irritation to the repressed, the fearful, the self-satisfied, and the incurious. His refusing to wear the hand-me-down clothes of outworn philosophies and creeds; his resolve to see the world afresh and to see it steadily from his own personal angle; his wry, unsleeping awareness of the ambivalences, the dark subtleties that plague the human soul: these will always make him suspect to the conformist taxpayer and his pitchmen in the universities and churches.

Where the conformist and his pitchmen cannot ignore the poet's words, they work to distort or emasculate them. I have yet to see Byron's and Shelley's rebellious lyrics in any school anthology of English poems. Or William Blake's. Thousands of students graduate each year from the nation's schools without ever learning that these poets were the fierce critics of the society they knew, of man's perennial viciousness and folly. What they wrote, what any poet has written, are poems – not literature! Literature is the revenge society takes on the poet, its muted polite hosannah over the fact that it has blunted his shafts and rendered them harmless. [. . .]

Blake was right; praise is the practice of art. Joy, fullness of feeling, is the core of the creative mystery. My dominant mood is that of ecstasy and gratitude. To have written even one poem that speaks with rhythmic authority about matters that are enduringly important is something to be immensely, reverently thankful for – and I am intoxicated enough to think I have written more than one. Why should I try to deceive anyone by false modesty? The sharp-nosed critics and the civilized few to whom these things still matter will ferret these poems out despite my efforts to hoodwink them. I was once asked: "Whom does the poet write for?" "For God," I answered.

But you're very welcome to eavesdrop.

("Foreword," *Collected Poems*, 1965)

* * *

Though my mother cursed obsessively and never, or seldom, praised me, I have one or two joyful memories. Every Monday morning during the summer months my mother went down to the Champ-de-Mars where the farmers from outlying villages marketed their produce. [. . .]

Ah, the delicious smells that wafted to me from the bags of potatoes, from the onion skins, and damp straw scattered underfoot. The dazzling array of colours, the white purity of cauliflower, the glossy robustness of tomatoes. I wanted to reach out and take their shine into my hand and walk off with it. The wonderful matter-of-factness of carrots and turnips, of the farmer's wagon, and patient horse standing in the shafts. And the people all around me, in crowds and bunches, the vigour and animation with which they moved and struck bargains. This, my young mind intuited, was what being alive meant: scramble, confusion, and disorder.

For all that I or anyone can tell, the Dionysian in me was born then and there. Thereafter, at great cost to me, I was to equate chaos with vitality, order and respectability with moribundity and stagnation. My life, no doubt, would have been a great deal easier had disorder not been accompanied by insight and rapture. At the time unaware, I was being given a standard by which to judge my own poetry and that of others. Poems, I have always believed, have to have the vitality and rough vigour of the marketplace. If I despise formalism and academic poetry, it's because I remember onions falling from their burlap sack and comically rolling down the cobbled hill and along the gutter, to be followed by an ambitious potato trying to catch up with them. Who knows what metaphors were spawned in my unconscious from seeing them race one another towards the gutter at the end of the short street?

(*Waiting for the Messiah*, 58–59, 1985)

* * *

A "rootless cosmopolite," I was aware of the large world beyond Canada's borders. The seminal influences, intellectual and cultural, came not from this country but from Europe. I read the poems of Mayakovsky and Yesenin, I didn't read those of Duncan Campbell Scott or E. J. Pratt. I read the novels of Gladkov and Ehrenburg, I didn't read those of Ralph Connor, and somehow the imperishable [Susanna Moodie] escaped my notice.

What was happening in Germany and Russia, in France and fascist Italy, seemed vastly more important to me than what was going on in Canada. Though war was about to break out in Spain and else-where, Canada was a sleeping pygmy. In the wintertime, a big white yawn. Neither the French Canadians nor the English Canadians impressed me unduly by their cultural achievements. Their parochial aspirations left me cold or indifferent. The French Canadians, their anti-Semitism fuelled by an ultramontanist Catholicism, seemed eternally mired in a medieval outlook. As for the Anglos, how could one expect Hitler's ominous speeches to take their apolitical minds away from the baseball playoffs at Yankee Stadium? [. . .]

The only exciting thing happening in Canada, apart from the annual rodeo show, was the creation of the Co-operative Common-wealth Federation. Its impetus was the Great Depression which lasted nearly the entire decade. Only with the outbreak of war in 1939 did the workers file back into the idle factories and the miners descend into their pits again. There's nothing wrong with capital-ism, said the radical know-it-alls, that a good war can't remedy. The CCF was a political party formed to advance the interests of the des-perate farmers and workers. Its first annual convention was held in Regina in 1933.

I felt myself to be a part of a world-wide movement for revolu-tionary change that was going to restructure society from top to bottom. The desired goal was peace, social justice, and the end of human alienation. I was conscious of a messianic purpose and experi-enced the liberating hubris that allows one to kill people with a clear conscience. For the first time in my life I was tasting this century's most intoxicating brew, the sense of power the conviction of infalli-bility gives one. Though not a Communist, I identified completely with Marx's messianic proletariat.

(*Waiting for the Messiah*, 155, 1985)

*   *   *

I had come upon Nietzsche long before I met [John] Sutherland, but I knew almost nothing about Lawrence. It was John and Audrey who made D. H. L. a reality for me. I began to read his poetry and fiction, his criticism, and indeed everything he wrote, with increasing astonishment and reverence. Lawrence despised English gentility and puritanism as much as I did. No writer, I felt, had his ear closer to the febrile heartbeat of our sick civilization than did Lawrence. He confirmed my outlook to such a degree that many times, when reading him, I felt spooked. I was completely at one with him in his philosophy of sex and views of Christianity. Lawrence's criticism of Christianity, particularly of its romanticism and sexual repressiveness, is every bit as forceful as Nietzsche's. For this reason, Lawrence, for me, became the archetypal anti-Canuck. And whenever I wished to give myself huge belly laughs, I imagined him walking the streets of Toronto or Calgary. As for the priest-ridden Québécois, it never occurred to me for a single moment that Lawrence could ever have a place in their thoughts or affections.

(*Waiting for the Messiah*, 223, 1985)

    *   *   *

Your trouble is the same as that of all my other reviewers – you look at me through Canadian eyes, with all the assumptions, prejudices, and (meaning no offence) provincialism of an educated Englishman. But I'm not really a Canadian, though I've lived here nearly all my life: I'm a European, and a Hebrew at that, much closer to France and Russia than I am to England. Which means that as a poet, spiritually and emotionally, I am more in tune with Heine, Baudelaire, Tuwim, and Pushkin than with any English poet you might name, except Byron who of course is the most European and cosmopolitan, the least insular, of the English poets.

(To Milton Wilson, 1 December 1958)

    *   *   *

The realization, after all my false starts and confusions, that I was a poet took a long time coming. Though I'd written many poems before, after I'd written "The Swimmer," there was no doubt in my mind. That happened in 1944. [. . .]

I headed up University towards St. Catherine then turned right and continued walking. I passed Child's restaurant (which is no longer there today), right near the Princess Theatre, which is still there but under another name. On a sudden impulse, I turned back and went into the restaurant, sat down, and ordered a cup of coffee. The waitress brought it to me and left it on my table without even glancing at me. I looked like a poor tipper. All of a sudden, a dazzling tumult of images came into my head and with them a tremendous excitement. I rose from my chair and signalled frantically to the waitress. When she was standing beside me, I grabbed the pencil out of her hand and was about to also grab her order pad when I seized a napkin instead, and, quite lost to everything going on around me, began writing furiously on it. Within five minutes an entire poem had written itself. I looked at it incredulously, as if it were a missive which the waitress, who had not moved away, had just handed to me.

It was "The Swimmer." That's just the way the poem happened. The premonitory excitement, the pell-mell rush of images, the inspired language, of which I didn't have to change more than a word or two. I looked at it and knew I had written my first major poem. I also knew with the same certainty I'd had an experience only a poet can have. Never before had I known such ecstasy, such release and joy, or felt my whole being concentrated with such intensity. That event convinced me that I was a poet. It was like hearing the voice of God. I had heard it as plainly as Moses had, as Abraham when the Lord bid him to light out for Canaan.

After that, there was no turning back. Nothing, after that experience, could shake my belief that someone up there had blessed or cursed me with the poet's vocation.

(*Waiting for the Messiah*, 227–29, 1985)

* * *

The origins of poems are obscure; only when the poet is uncommonly self-analytical can he trace the beginnings, the obscure urges or irritations, behind the finished work. For myself, I find when I'm really "hot" that the commencement of a poem takes place with a rush of images to my head which I put down on paper as swiftly as they occur. When the stream stops coming I look at what I've written and try to decipher as best I can what it is that my "unconscious" is trying to tell me and only when I detect some pattern trying to realize itself to my mind do I sit down to the actual composition of the poem. The quality of irony which you rightly detect in the poem is the self-ironic smile of a man who sees the drift of the joke – and sees that the joke is on him. But all irony in poetry, I believe, is the consequence of the two antithetical roles the poet embraces, that of passionate participant and detached observer. It springs from his ability to keep a number – the more the better – of contradictory thoughts and emotions in suspension. A really good poet is capable of going off vigorously in several directions at once. I do not say he does, only that he's capable of doing so. The distinction is important.

(To Robert Creeley, 26 May 1953)

* * *

. . . although as a rule I leave theorizing about poetry to others, there are one or two work-a-day rules I try to govern myself by when writing verse. For me, rhythm and imagery usually tell the story; I'm not much interested in any poet's ideas unless he can make them dance for me, that is embody them in a rhythmic pattern of visual images, which is only another way of saying the same thing in different words. If I want sociology, economics, uplift, or metaphysics, or that generalized state of despairing benevolence concerning the prospects of the human race which seems to characterize much of present-day poetic effort, I know my way around a library as well as the next man. Catalogues are no mystery to me. I regard the writing of verse as a serious craft, the most serious there is, demanding from a man everything he's got. Moreover, it's a craft in which good intentions count for nil. It's how much a man has absorbed into his being that counts, how he opens up continuously to experience, and then with talent and luck communicates to others without fuss or fanfare or affectation, but sincerely, honestly, simply. . . .

(Letter to Cid Corman, *Origin* [Autumn 1954].)

* * *

I'm glad "Cain" pleases you. You go to the core of the poems as unerringly as you've gone to others. For me, the problem of Cain is just this – the assertion of the human will against life itself. I got the idea when I re-read the story in *Genesis* last summer, and I understood better than I had ever before that the problem of Cain was the problem of the human race. God, you will remember, never addresses so much as a syllable to Abel; it is to Cain, and to Cain alone, that he speaks. Not the victim, but the victimizer is His problem; not the innocent, but the guilty. Man can only live by shedding blood – and he has his conscience against him. What a dilemma.

Now I've just finished another longish poem entitled: "For Mao Tse Tung: A Meditation on Flies and Kings." I can't decide whether it's the best poem I've written, or the worst. That, too, is a dilemma, I suppose! It's an anti-Christian poem, rejecting the ethic of compassion and suffering and embracing instead heroic joy – the great are they who forge personal values of courage and exuberance in the face of emptiness and annihilation – the tragic wheel of necessity, for which fire is my symbol.

(To Milton Wilson, 7 August 1958)

* * *

My own version of "Tall Man Executes a Jig" goes something like this. Chaos surrounds us, in the beginning as now, symbolized by the inexplicable gnats ("Fruitflies he'd call them except there was no fruit about"). But the chaos also has within it a principle of creativity, the gnats that leave their "orthodox unrest" to seek out the hairs in the tall man's arms. They suffer in their confinement, but to him their strugglings appear like purest joy. From this principle of creativity evolves man at his highest and best, at his most creative. As artist, thinker, and lover. But the dark chaos with pain and evil still surrounds him; and the bee instinctively making his wonderful structures leaves him disdainfully to his confusions. A possible answer to evil is renunciation, oriental and Christian (Note the play on the word *sun*). Is that the revelation? The second movement of Beethoven's Ninth. And I make the same answer he does. NO. What about Judaic optimism then? The arm of Moses against the stricken sun. The world is good, bless the Creator. Hallelujah. Ha, but what's this that I see at my feet? A poor violated grass-snake which becomes the symbol for the pain and suffering that all sentient things must endure. My obsession, as by now you know. Stricken, robbed of his pride, the snake now invites us to curse the world, and the tall man is tempted to do so. But *adam*ant and fierce, he does not. Instead he lies down in fellowship of death with the rigid grass-snake (I intended the sexual irony you noted: Eros–Thanatos) and with all life from the very beginnings. But of all other living creatures nothing remains, death is the end for them: of perished badgers and racoons the claws alone remain, gripping the earth. Mere existence. Man alone transforms his extinction into art. That is his true resurrection; and in that resurrection, all living creatures share. The snake becomes my grand symbol for the imagination; coiling above the now "weary man's" head, it is his last halo, but it also suggests something menacing, since the resurrected snake has both pride and malice or vituperation (He wants to make the night bright with *his* stars, and tries to blot out the moon by blowing wreaths of cloud against it.) It is only love that resolves momentarily all the antinomies in a flash of light. But then the sky is "emptied."

(To Milton Wilson, 16 December 1961)

* * *

"Elephant"
I always wanted to write a poem that would express what I feel is the true relationship between art and reality along with my un-mad view concerning the nature of the poet. In fact, an *ars poetica* sans fuss, sans didactic eye-poking or ear-bashing. The vision of an elephant, one rainy afternoon when I found shelter in a deserted wayside shrine, scraping himself against a dark Nepalese tree, offered me the necessary symbol; enabled me to pack it into living and magnificent literal flesh, which is how I like to see my symbols march out of my brain into the marketplace. In poetry concreteness is all, what in another place I've called "sensuous vitality." Without that and the gift for metaphor, the would-be poet had better think of other employment. What's wrong with running a whorehouse nowadays? It's more honest, certainly more profitable, than turning out stillborn verse no amount of vigorous whacking and thwacking will make emit the cry of life. Yes, and add "musical delight which is the gift of the imagination" (Coleridge's epiphany). "Elephant" has all these elements, I think.

("Elephant," in *How Do I Love Thee*, ed. John Robert Colombo, 1970.)

* * *

But the contemporary poet must find some way into the living, fermenting core of the present. He cannot be merely an observer, otherwise what he says will be insignificant and unmoving. The problem for the Canadian poet is a very difficult one. He's removed from the great issues of the day: his dilemmas are unimportant and derivative. He cannot know the men of action, the movers and shakers of history, as Shakespeare knew the Raleighs and Essexes – certainly not on the college campus! History and geography have both condemned him to be a minor poet. To allow himself to be pushed gently into a quiet pool in which he makes small fin-splashes seems to be his fate.

The fact is, merely to keep afloat the Canadian poet has to thrash about in the water. "I go about making trouble for myself." Since there are no great issues and no great passions, I've had to make them or rather fake them. Minor, insignificant quarrels I've deliberately blown up to give myself the illusion that I was participating in some mighty movement of history. Emotionally, this is a country where one can go quickly to sleep. How to simulate in himself the emotions of hate, disgust, loathing, anger, and so on: that's the problem of the Canadian poet. If he doesn't he finds himself saying beautiful nothings – blabbermouthing.

(To Milton Wilson, 9 June 1963)

* * *

Yesterday I took out of the library Ilya Ehrenburg's memoirs of the first years of the revolution and I'm enjoying it hugely. It mainly deals with the writers whom he knew at the time, Blok and Babel and Pasternak and many, many others. He gives vivid pen portraits of them and he's got the novelist's eye for the telling detail. I'm glad I found the book in the local library because it's given me the perfect epigraph for my new book, the one I finished this summer and which I've titled *The Tightrope Dancer*. It's something Tsvetayeva said or wrote: "Ghetto of the elect. A wall, a ditch. Expect no mercy. In this most Christian of worlds poets are Jews."

[. . .] I see the poet as dancing on a rope that is stretched tautly between sexuality and death. The distinction between the major poet and the minor one is that the former dances on the tightrope while the other walks carefully across it. Of course you can see where the critic fits in: he's the fellow with the binoculars watching the performance on the tightrope from a secure position on the ground. It was great having Bill [Goodwin] with me for we had many interesting seminars on our beach on women, sex, politics, marriage and what a crocodile's testicles looked like. Many of my poems came directly out of conversations or were begun by a remark either one of us may have made. [. . .]

(To Musia Schwartz, 24 August 1977)

* * *

Western civilization seems to be enveloped in a Freudian sadness that assumes the world has become one vast sanitarium or hospital.

For a large number of people life has lost its savour and zest. The joy of living has gone out of them. They are weighed down by inexpressible cares and worries; they are repressed, anxious, and suffer from feelings of unreality.

It is for these frightened, alienated, unhappy people in Western society that the modern poet speaks. He is their voice, their champion and protector. For they, along with himself, are the internal exiles in a world that has forgotten what it is to be human. Where is the love and laughter and joy that should be the birthright of every human being? Where, indeed, is that abundant life once promised to us by the founders of the Christian religion and by the architects of the liberal, progressive state? It lies in ruins on the analyst's couch.

Is the free, spontaneous unfolding of the individual possible in a technological society that has alienated him from nature and from his fellow-men? Is it possible in a society that asks him to surrender his human dignity to idols more gruesome than ever Moloch and Baal were? I do not think so. Of course, as of old, we still worship Mammon but we immolate ourselves daily before the even more destructive and terrifying idols of Speed, Power, Status, and Public Opinion.

Poetry opposes the totality of the self to the creeping totalitarianism of the twentieth century. The pressures on the individual to simplify and abstract, to deaden his senses, and to live either in his brains or his loins, are becoming more and more difficult to withstand and resist. In the face of these pressures, poetry affirms that life must be enjoyed in all its delicious complexity. It says to the harassed men and women of today: you must live fully and experience all that you can; only in that way will you be living humanly. A great poet said it a long time ago: we must all be born again. Modern life, with its specialization and division of labour, is turning each of us into anatomical and physiological fragments – a brain, an eye, a nose, an arm, or a leg. We must somehow find a way to re-assemble these into a human being. I believe that the reading and writing of poetry is a necessary start in the process of reassembling.

There is no force more subversive than poetry and that is why tyrants have always feared it and sought to suppress it. But not only tyrants. Everyone who has a vested interest in preventing the individual from discovering the truth of his own self and his own capacities fears the liberating power that resides in poetry. Old and crippling creeds, suffocating conventions, the dishonest rationalizations and hypocrisies the defeated and joyless put forward in the name of virtue – to all these poetry turns a smiling, disdainful countenance.

Wise men have said the truth shall make you free. Yes, poetic truth – an awareness of the many-sided nature of Being that wars eternally against all metaphysical and political constructions claiming to free men from the need to doubt and explore.

A poem is an Alka-Seltzer tablet: orthodoxies begin to fizz when one is dropped into their midst. Distrustful of abstractions, poetry is in love with the concrete and the particular. It has something more important to do than to manufacture pretty baubles for pedants and culture-Philistines or for timorous spinsters and school-marms with a turn for verse. When he hears these people exclaim rhapsodically: "How beautiful!" the true poet takes to his heels and makes for the nearest lavatory.

("Poets: The Conscience of Mankind," *The Globe Magazine*, 15 June 1963)

A NOTE ON THE TEXT

The poems were selected and arranged by Irving Layton with the help of Dennis Lee (the 1982 edition) and with Sam Solecki (1989). With the exception of the introduction, the prose selections from Irving Layton's writings, the typographical design, and the silent correction of typographical errors, this edition follows in all other aspects the 1982 and the 1989 editions.

INDEX OF TITLES

(See opposite for listing of title abbreviations)

IRVING LAYTON was born in 1912 and has lived most of his life in Montreal. One of Canada's most highly celebrated and prolific poets, having authored over forty books of poetry, many of which have appeared in translation, Layton has been the recipient of numerous awards for his poetry and for his contribution to Canadian literature. He was nominated twice for the Nobel Prize for Literature.